What the reviewers said:

This is a wonderful book that should be read by everyone who thinks that theology cannot address the issues with which so many of us are preoccupied in the 'ordinary-ness' of our lives: as people who commute and exercise and worry about diet and have a hard time sleeping. Robert Banks shows us that to think theologically can be a very exciting activity of bringing the riches of divine revelation to bear on the complexities of our lives.

Dr Richard Mouw
Professor of Christian Philosophy
and Ethics
Fuller Theological Seminary
Pasadena, California, USA

Theology is far too important to be left to the theologians! Robert Banks, though himself a very distinguished theologian, seeks to recover a theology *of* the people of God *for* the people of God and encourages us in our high calling to *do* theology as well as talk about it. In my opinion, this is the best book on grassroots theology that is currently available. There is much more to be said, but I cannot think of a better place for laity or clergy to begin thinking about the subject. It should be required reading for all theological students (and their teachers).

W. Ward Gasque
The E. Marshall Sheppard Professor
of Biblical Studies,
Regent College,
Vancouver, Canada

ROBERT BANKS

ALL THE BUSINESS
OF LIFE

Bringing Theology Down to Earth

AN ALBATROSS BOOK

© Robert Banks 1987

Published in Australia and New Zealand by
Albatross Books Pty Ltd
PO Box 320, Sutherland
NSW 2232, Australia
in the United States of America by
Albatross Books
PO Box 131, Claremont
CA 91711, USA
and in the United Kingdom by
Lion Publishing
Sandy Lane West, Littlemore
Oxford, England

First edition 1987
Second edition 1989

National Library of Australia
Cataloguing-in-Publication data

   Banks, Robert, 1939–
      All the business of life

      ISBN 0 86760 039 X (Albatross)
      ISBN 0 7459 1295 8 (Lion)

      1. Christian life — 1960 –
      I. Title

   248.4

Cover photo: The Photo Library, North Sydney
Typeset by Rochester Communications Group, Sydney
Printed by Singapore National Printers

Contents

To
Peter, Julie, Katie and Stephen
for our various conversations on the subject
and
David, Lynlea and Andrew
for reading and commenting on the manuscript
and to
Ken
for his work in editing the book

1

An intellectual pilgrimage

ALMOST TWENTY-FIVE YEARS AGO my wife and I were visited by a staff member from the seminary we had recently attended. Having just joined the staff of a large city church in another state, we were pleased to see a well-known face. To thank us for our hospitality, he left us a book called *Christian Devotion* by a well-known Scottish author, John Baillie, which contained a chapter with the unusual title 'A Theology of Sleep'. Was this a serious title or was the writer just catching our attention? After quoting Psalm 127:1-2, he introduced the subject in the following way:

> My subject is the theology of sleep. It is an unusual subject, but I make no apology for it. I think we hear far too few sermons about sleep. After all, we spend a very large share of our lives sleeping. I suppose that on average I've slept for eight hours out of every twenty-four during the whole of my life, and that means I've slept for well over twenty years... Don't you agree then that the Christian gospel should have something to say about the sleeping third of our lives as well as about the waking two-thirds of them? I believe it has something to say and that this text serves as a good beginning for the exposition of it.[1]

Baillie's juxtaposition of 'theology' with something as mundane as 'sleep' came as a shock. Theology only dealt

---

1. J. Baillie, *Christian Devotion*, Oxford University Press, 1962, p.70

with those lofty themes arising out of God's plan of salvation! How could so routine — and unconscious — an activity as sleep have anything to do with it? But the more I thought about it the more I was convinced. Did not the Bible encourage us to view all our activities and responsibilities in the light of Christ? If so, then it was proper to preach and teach on such a matter. And if it was proper to do this, then theology should help clarify what should be said.

At the time I did not see the implications of what Baillie was saying for systematic Christian thinking and all the business of life. If there was some link between believing and sleeping, then I should start connecting up my basic convictions with many other areas of life that I had previously taken for granted. While I had long believed in principle that Christianity should affect the whole of one's life, I had not appreciated how wide-ranging or deep-thinking an obligation that was. Nor did I sense at the time that Baillie's remarks might lead to further questions about the whole enterprise of theology. In fact, so pressured was our life during our time at the city church that I was not even able to put into practice what he said about sleeping!

I would not claim to see the full implications of what he was saying even now. But gradually I have become aware of what some of those are. This was not a purely intellectual affair: only as I listened to others' difficulties and worked through some personal dilemmas did I begin to appreciate what was involved.

Scenes from everyday life

To explain the practical outworkings of this basic insight, it is appropriate to start with some stories rather than statements. The Bible itself, the basis of the Christian faith, is largely a series of stories. Much of its relevance comes from that. The best stories, whether personal ones or those of other people, have a way of focussing on the issue. We also tend to identify with them more easily. I begin with several stories told to me by people I know. These people are by no means untypical. I follow their stories with part of my own, since this explains what led me to write this book.

The following stories occurred in a relatively short space of time to people who belonged to the same small group. I wish I had taken down their stories verbatim so that I could let them speak in their own words. But even they have difficulty now putting themselves back fully into the situations they described. To protect the anonymity of those involved, I have changed certain details of age, name and even sex.

1. Chris: a work-related problem
I have known Chris for more than ten years. We first met when I was still teaching in a university and she was in her early twenties. A few months after we had moved to Canberra we met up again, not socially this time but in a more personal way. Chris is quietly-spoken, outgoing and a real 'people person'. She has a good sense of humour and enjoys playing sport. Several years after I first met her she married, though it was not till after the problem I am about to relate that she had her first child.

She is a graduate in economics and works for a large fast-growing computer company. At the time of the particular problem I want to relate she was climbing through the ranks to more responsible positions and had just entered middle-management with a number of people under her supervision. She had not gone out of her way to seek promotions, being content to master each job she had been given and stay in it until her superiors encouraged her to apply for a new situation.

Chris is married to Tom, a schoolteacher who gets home around three-thirty in the afternoon and is therefore able to help more with domestic responsibilities, a task he enjoys. The only problem with their dual working patterns stemmed from occasional bouts of sickness Tom suffered which sometimes kept him in bed for several days at a time. Chris felt badly when these illnesses came and occasionally took time off from her work to look after Tom.

However, because of the growing volume of work, Chris was under pressure to work longer hours. By arrangement, normally she could leave work around four o'clock and be home half-an-hour later. But then she found she was often staying back at work for an hour or two extra, placing extra pressure upon Tom in the home at meal time. It also meant less time together. However, others in the firm, and especially her boss, were tending to work back even longer, all without receiving any additional wages. Chris felt a real responsibility to her section and also felt guilty at not putting in as much time as others. Though it did not rank highly with her, she knew that further promotional prospects were possibly tied to others' estimates of her commitment to the job.

When we discussed the matter Chris admitted that part of the reason for her wanting to stay back was the attitude she had to work. For example, her boss sometimes passed on work to her from senior management that was marked urgent. But she had been in the firm long enough to know that if left for a couple of weeks some of this would become redundant. Yet she found it difficult to engage in deliberate delaying tactics and there was always the chance that she would set aside the wrong item. Chris has always prided herself on doing her work thoroughly, but if she continued to try and do everything asked of her, and do it thoroughly or in time, she would have to remain longer at her desk.

There was a further problem. Chris has always been sensitive to other people's problems and a good listener. Discerning this, some of her colleagues discussed their problems with her from time to time. Even her boss did, finding her a helpful sounding board for some of his anxieties. Chris saw these conversations as a real contribution. But giving attention to people in this way left her even less time to finish the work on her desk. In any case, Chris wanted to give more time to the people in her church and found this suffering because of the extra time she had to spend at work.

Chris' dilemma is not uncommon. Put yourself in her shoes and ask what she should do in this situation. With respect to hours of work, should she keep generally to the legal number of hours she was contracted to work or regularly stay back longer when her work is getting behind? Is her first duty to her husband and daughter, even though she has less time at home with her increased office responsibilities than most people do in such a job? What balance should she seek to achieve between work and her family responsibilities, not to speak of her love of sport? Should she yield to the pressure to stay longer at work out of a sense of responsibility to her colleagues or to increase her chances of gaining a more responsible position? How much is the problem basically the company's rather than hers because of the pressures and expectations it loads upon her?

Further, how much should she have excellence or thoroughness as her goal? In other words, how Christian are these values or how manipulated are they by employers to their own ends? And how feasible are either of them in the pressured working conditions imposed on most employees? Where thoroughness and deadlines come into conflict, is it better to do everything partially well or only certain things fully well? Should she make it a priority not to jeopardise her chances of promotion so that she can later exercise a greater influence upon the way the company operates or should this not be one of her concerns? How obligated is Chris to follow all her superior's instructions or example? Should she confront her superior with the tensions she is experiencing and ask for a fairer deal?

More generally, what produces the present work situation which puts people under such pressure and should not companies do something about it? Do they not have a responsibility to ensure that work remains humane, even at the expense of productivity? How much responsibility do superiors have to work at a pace and length that does not exert pressure upon their subordinates? Should not job descriptions take account of time employees spend on interpersonal matters which may significantly affect both productivity and morale? What is the personal and social cost, even the ultimate eco-

nomic cost, of energy not spent at home deepening relationships and strengthening family life?

2. Martin: a leisure-time dilemma

My friendship with Martin goes back even further than my
contact with Chris. He and his wife, at that stage childless,
had just moved to Canberra and were having difficulty settling into church life. Martin thinks a lot and is often quite
outspoken in what he says. He also keeps himself physically
in good shape and is a keen sportsman. Although he is a
junior executive in a major industrial organisation, he continues to find time to play tennis one night a week in winter
and cricket on Saturdays in the summer months. His wife is
agreeable to this, knowing how much it means to him and
how much it balances his responsibilities at work.

In his cricket team Martin is regarded as one of the better
players. Unlike the majority of members, he has taken an
interest in wider aspects of the game. He has sat on planning
committees which both arrange the fixtures and discuss
other matters, such as relegation. For a time he was con-
venor of a discipline committee which discussed the interpretation of rules and complaints about unfair play. Quite apart
from his cricketing abilities and willingness to take on
administrative responsibilities, Martin is generally well
regarded by the members of his team.

Over the past few years he has observed an increasing
deterioration in players' attitudes to the game. There is far
more abuse of batsmen by the fielding side while the game
is in progress. This unsettles the player and renders him
more vulnerable. There are more attempts to deceive the
umpire through unjustified appeals around the crease or
false information about whether balls have crossed the
boundary line. The view that one should win at all costs also
appears to be gaining ground: this means that rules, like
speed limits, do not matter so long as you are not found out.
At times this behaviour enables his team to win when it
should have lost. He sees other teams moving in the same

direction and is aware that junior teams are being inculcated in the same spirit. Since he loves cricket as a game, it troubles him to see standards dropping. It seems to him a betrayal of what the game is all about and he is concerned for its future.

In an attempt to do something about this state of affairs, Martin raised the issue with some of the main offenders in his team. This did not lead to any change. He also brought the matter up at a team meeting, but received no guarantee that things would alter. What should he do next? He could remain in the team, hoping that his own standard of play and occasional raising of the issue might eventually lead to change. But he was pessimistic about this. He could demote himself and join a team from a lower division in his club where more respect was still given to the rules. This would take a lot of enjoyment out of his game. As a last resort he could retire from cricket altogether. Yet this would cause him great disappointment.

Martin's dilemma may have been a very specific one, but it involves a whole set of major concerns. Once again place yourself in the situation in which he found himself. Having raised the issue with the team, does he bear responsibility for the team's decision to continue with its approach to the game? To what extent is personal integrity compromised by corporate behaviour? How much would his leaving the team deprive it of a challenge that might prevent its standards from deteriorating even further? Is his personal enjoyment of the game at this upper division level something he should be prepared to sacrifice for the sake of ethical integrity?

There are other issues. For example, should he be giving so much time to the game when it means leaving his wife to look after their three young children for another half day a week, even if she is fully agreeable to this and they often come to the match? Or does not the physically confined nature of his work during the week and his innate sporting ability require some such outlet as he has found? How important is it to encourage people like Martin to continue participating in games when so many people these days have become merely spectators?

Beyond this, how much has the professionalisation and commercialisation of cricket adversely affected the standards of the game and whose responsibility is it to do something about this? What obligation do leading sports personalities, especially the Christians among them, have to counter the 'win at all costs' mentality that so easily takes over? How can the predominance of international, national and regional sporting events over local ones be reduced so that there is more participation on the part of ordinary people? Should Christians in particular be promoting non-competitive games as an antidote to the takeover of leisure by the same spirit that pervades the work environment? Is there something inherent in our highly commercial and competitive society that leads to the transformation even of games into simulations of the work situation and what can be done about this?

3. Jan: a role-definition dilemma

Jan is in her early thirties and has four small children. These were born less than a year apart and the youngest has just turned three. After she completed her university degree, she worked as an interior decorator, mostly advising large companies and businesses on office decor. She was extremely good at her job and was highly regarded by her employers. But during the last seven years, motherhood and housework has been a more than full-time occupation. We have known Jan for nearly fifteen years and my wife in particular has had a lot to do with her. Jan is a very capable person, with independent opinions and an extremely practical approach to life. She is also a no-nonsense person and has a strong sense of living by her values.

Ian, her husband, is involved in a small but growing legal practice and has recently been made a partner. Though he has tried to take his family responsibilities seriously, the sudden growth of the company and his new position have made heavy demands upon him. Until the past few months he has demands upon him. Until the past few months he has resisted any pressures to take work home with him. At times he now finds this difficult to avoid. As a number of his clients have interstate interests, he has to make regular trips to other cities, sometimes being away for two or three nights at a time. He tries to make up for this by keeping holidays scrupulously free and taking long breaks whenever possible.

Allow me to take you back to the situation Jan was in at the time she talked about her dilemma. Some of you will identify with her. Enter into her situation as it was then and consider how you would approach it yourself. Jan has reached the point where the last of the children will begin pre-school. She has been entering into a new period of freedom gradually over the last two years and is looking forward to it with considerable anticipation. There are some books she has always wanted to read. There are people with whom she would like to spend more time. There are one or two practical courses she is thinking of taking. She also takes prayer seriously and would like to have more leisure for it.

There are pressures working against this happening. She still has a lot of housework, shopping and family co-ordinating to do which she does not mind greatly, but at times it gets her down. Not only is it repetitive, but when there is sickness in the house, as there frequently seems to be, she has to abandon most of her plans. Ian's regular absences have also put pressure on the free time she is beginning to experience.

A number of her friends who have moved back into the workforce assume that she will return to work the moment her youngest child is in pre-school. These friends constantly talk about the need to fulfil oneself through meaningful employment. They also point out the greater financial independence this would give her. They tend to regard anyone who stays at home as in danger of becoming a vegetable. Jan feels the pressure of their attitude and wonders whether she will have enough social interaction and intellectual stimulation if she does not go back to work.

There are other factors to consider. While ideally she would prefer to remain at home, almost all the people her age in her neighbourhood now have jobs. She feels rather lonely at times, particularly when her husband is away. The people closest to her in her church live across town, too far to drop in on in a casual way. Her extended family lives in another city and in any case relations with some of its members are strained. She does have informal links with a voluntary welfare agency, which would like her to do some unpaid part-time work. But she would have to be careful that this did not surreptitiously claim more time than she wishes to give.

What then should she do? Is it possible that she could make the nurturing of her children and the deepening of the relationship with her husband her main vocation, yet become fulfilled and liberated in the way she believes a person should be? If so, can she combine this with part-time voluntary work, even though this might intermittently encroach upon time she would like to give to reading, visiting and taking an occasional course? Although she would meet people by doing some of these things, how does she avoid the problem of loneliness while she is at home? She wonders where she will draw the strength from to resist the pressures of her friends who are employed full-time.

There are other issues. Would the lengthy periods of time she devotes to housework, shopping and related chores become more satisfying if she could find a a deeper purpose in these activities? How does she handle the fatigue that mothering and domestic work induces, especially in relation to prayer and meditation which often require more energy than she has available? Given the busyness of her closest friends, how can she spend enough time with them to maintain and deepen their relationship?

Underlying some of these queries are a number of very serious social issues. For example, what are the main factors eroding relationships in the modern city and how can they be combatted? How can cities be planned so as to make suburbs less isolated from the most dynamic centres of their life?

Should companies be obliged to make up time to familes that is taken from them by their employees having to travel on their behalf? How important or feasible is it for churches to restructure themselves so they can develop a degree of neighbourliness in the increasingly deserted suburbs of the modern city?

4. Neil and Sue: a life-stage decision

I would also like to introduce you to Neil and Sue. We have not known them as long as we have the others, but our links now go back some time. Neil is in his late thirties and comes from a lower middle-class background, as does his wife. They were married in their late teens. The elder of their two sons has a job as an apprentice and the younger has left school and is at present unemployed. Some years ago they had to move from the city where they were married.

Sue and Neil were both influenced by the counter-culture movement in the late sixties and early seventies, before they met as well as afterwards. Both had become members of a Christian community and were attracted to the simple lifestyle. Neil had also spent time in a Third World country and was deeply affected by what he encountered. It was shortly after his return that he and Sue met.

Neil and Sue were at a crossroads in their lives. For most of his working life Neil has worked as a projectionist in a theatre. The work has not always been regular, the hours are difficult and he has often found his job monotonous. To supplement his income, and to help pay off the mortgage on their home, Sue took a part-time job in a welfare agency. Although they live in an older timber cottage in one of the poorer parts of the city, they found they did not have much money to spare.

Outside his employment, Neil loves to work with his hands. He has considerable skill as a potter, but has little time to give to this interest. For a long time he has dreamt about taking up craft as a full-time activity. He knows that such a decision would involve financial struggle for a time, but believes he could eventually make a living from his craft-work. Sue has encouraged both his interest in pottery and dream of an alternative occupation. Secretly, however, she is concerned about their future security, especially as her job with the welfare agency is vulnerable to government cut-backs. She is also aware that Neil would need additional equipment in order to do his work properly and that it would take some time before he could establish a clientele for his craftwork. Also, if things did not work out, it is clear that once Neil has resigned his projectionist position, there is very little likelihood he could regain it.

Any such move raises a number of difficult issues. How much should we expect our employment to be related to our creative capacities? How much should we be willing under God to take risks, both for ourselves and our families, in choosing an occupation? How much should a concern for security be a factor? At what stage in life can major changes of this kind be most effectively made?

There are other questions. What responsibility does the local church have to a person or family in this position? If the church encourages a move in a new direction, does it have an obligation to help out financially until the new line of work is reasonably established? How far should the church be challenging its people generally to explore new types and patterns of work and so help overcome the problem of meaningless work or unemployment in our society?

What is the nature and purpose of work anyway? How satisfactory are the present modes, choices and structures of work? In a society from which full employment has probably gone forever, how much responsibility rests upon govern-ment and other institutions to redefine work or place less emphasis upon its contribution to society? In what ways do we need an alteration in attitudes to and conditions of work so that jobs can become more suitable and meaningful? Which companies, departments and organisations are going to provide the models for this? These are only some of the broader issues that Neil and Sue's dilemma raises.

Stages on a personal journey
Once upon a time

Listening to experiences such as these over the years helped me to see how little theology had to say to many Christians' dilemmas. Meanwhile changes in my own life and thinking were forcing me in the same direction. Let me return again to the large city church I referred to earlier. Sometimes I shudder to think of some of the sermons I preached and some of the advice that I gave. For example, talks on the need for an early morning 'quiet time' that took no account of the plight of young mothers whose small children woke up before six and whose husbands left home around seven. Or talks about commitment which centred on what people could do by way of work for the church rather than how they could fulfil their vocation through their work.

But gradually I began to recognise some of the pressures our hyperactive and overly organised church placed upon its members. Indeed, I started to feel the physical and family effects of some of these myself. My wife was even more aware of these than I was. Alongside some post-graduate study I was doing, I gave some time to thinking about these practical concerns and their implications for Christian living. In fact it was partly in order to clear more time for this, that two years later we left the church so that I could do further study overseas.

At the time I did not fully understand that concerns as practical as the ones that were troubling me could become the main focus of my thesis. Working through the pressing question of the church and ministry remained a sideline for me during the next four years, though one that was to result in significant changes. Still, my research into Jesus' ethics, especially his attitude to the Law, arose from another personal issue with which I had been wrestling: the tension between obligation and freedom in daily Christian life.

During this time I was also assisting in a working-class congregation in Cambridge. This experience sharpened my questions about the nature and relevance of the church. As a result, the practical concern that had been a sideline for me so far as study was concerned increasingly assumed chief importance.

There were many sides to the problems I was having in this area. One was the distinction between clergy and laity. Slowly I came to see how much the former separated those who were ordained from the people around us as well as from the realities of ordinary life. Another was the large-scale bureaucratisation of the church. I came to realise how much the latter separated the church as a whole from the society in which it was set. For all my efforts to bridge these gaps, I did not seem to be able to do so effectively. I also had difficulties with much of the formality and inflexibility of meetings for church. After a long period of uncertainty, for these and other reasons I eventually withdrew from the ordained ministry. This was a very painful affair, not only because I was leaving behind something that had meant so much to me, but because it was hard to know what to do about the problems I had encountered.

Working through this question began to change the way I was thinking about theology itself. Shortly after the decision to leave the ordained ministry, I wrote to a friend back home. In the letter I made the following remarks:

I feel that I've spent the last ten years in a kind of ecclesiastical and theological ghetto. Although I used to have a real interest in the world around me and tried hard to understand it, since I began studying for the ministry increasingly I seem to have lost touch with it. The only way I can think of righting the balance would be to spend the next ten years in a secular setting renewing contact with the ideas, movements and values that shape the world around us. How can I ever contribute anything of value to that world from a thoughtful Christian point of view unless I have some understanding of what its concerns are and can begin to speak relevantly to it?

Entering a period of transition

Shortly after I wrote that letter, a possibility opened up for me to do just what I had suggested. Out of the blue I gained a five-year position in a research school of social sciences and was able to work on some of the key figures and movements that have shaped contemporary attitudes and structures.

This was followed by a five-year teaching position in a history department at another university. There I became more and more interested in the everyday first-century setting of the ideas and activities of the earliest Christians — economic, social, political and cultural — and in the rise and impact of the main secular world-views and movements on contemporary life over the last two centuries.

In both these places, my wife and I began to discover a more communal and down-to-earth church life. In these home churches I saw at first hand the enormous capacity all Christians have for engaging in mutual ministry. I also learned how they were able to work through many of their everyday concerns, dilemmas and responsibilities.

It was during this time that I wrote about Paul's idea of community, hoping to alert Christians to the challenge of Paul's highly participatory and down-to-earth view of the church. For him, church was essentially a people's affair and everyone had a vital part to play in every aspect of its life. To his mind, church was also about everyday concerns as much as anything else and this gave to the gatherings a highly practical air. Troubled by the fact that this book would only reach a limited audience, I decided to try my hand, somewhat inexpertly, at writing a small narrative about going to church in the first century. This little exercise persuaded me that any attempt to bring theology 'down-to-earth' had to have as great a concern for form as for content.

During my time in both the posts I have mentioned I was also beginning to think more seriously about certain every-day concerns. For example, how I and my family could cope with the increasing demands upon our time by a variety of people and organisations, what our responsibility was to the small street neighbourhood to which we belonged and what we should do with those creative gifts and personal interests we both had.

About this time, some ten years ago now, I was browsing through a bookshop and I came across a copy of Freud's work, *The Psychopathology of Everyday Life*. The reference to everyday life in Freud's title reminded me of Baillie's address on the theology of sleep that we had read almost fifteen years before. Then and there it occurred to me that what we needed was a wide-ranging 'theology of everyday life', one that would give as sustained attention to the issues of daily living as to the traditional subjects of theological reflection.

A year or two later, while on sabbatical, it became clear that we were facing a change of direction. So we entered into a more independent existence, one rooted in the home churches with which we had been involved and linked with certain interdenominational organisations attempting more generally to relate Christianity to Australian society.

And so to the present

What form does this way of life take? Sometimes my work is with occupational or student groups who are trying to work out how their faith should affect the work they are doing or preparing for and the institutions in which they are or will be doing it. Where such groups are made up of students this involves alerting them to the vocational responsibilities and dilemmas that one day they are going to face. Sometimes I am in the company of people hovering between belief and unbelief, many of whose dilemmas I find arise from their practical experience of life rather than intellectual objections.

My wife and I also spend time with groups of people who wish to identify, work through and confront some of the pervasive forces that shape so much of our daily lives. Many people feel oppressed by — and are looking for a Christian perspective upon — the pressures of time, change and mobility or feel powerless in the face of bureaucratic regulation or professional takeover of many parts of their lives. They wish to be liberated from these and indeed it is powers such as these, along with others relevant to more disadvantaged groups in our society, that should provide the agenda of a theology of liberation for our own context. Frequently, together with others, we give extended time to congregations and other Christian groups, encouraging them to develop their full potential for mutual ministry and support and suggesting how they might better relate their faith to all the areas of life in which they are engaged.

In these matters we have had a definite commitment to the city in which we live: not just in the sense of a staying in it rather than moving on at some point, but in the sense of learning about it, sharing in its life and actively seeking its welfare. The commitment extends to our immediate surroundings, both residents and environment — even to our own block of land. Such a commitment has involved us at times in struggles with the bureaucracy, resistance to land-developers, support of public transport and stimulating a sense of street (or in our case cul-de-sac) community.

Most of the writing I have done over the past ten years has its basis in one or other of the activities I have mentioned. A symposium on private values and public policy arose out of a four-year working group made up of senior public servants. We sought to discover how far fundamental Christian beliefs should or could inform decision-making in government administration. Writing about the tyranny of time had its origins in the problems my family and others had in this area; while *The Church Comes Home*, written together with my wife, is an extension of our efforts to help the churches establish such groups so that all Christians might take greater responsibility for their lives.

Over the past few years we have also been grappling with an underlying issue. If all Christians have a responsibility to bring their deepest convictions into contact with their most everyday concerns, what are the most effective ways of doing this? Are the learning structures in our congregations, para-church groups, colleges and seminaries equipping us adequately? The more we have struggled with this issue, the more convinced we have become that, however far present structures can take us, we need alternative approaches as well.

In describing some of my own pilgrimage in understanding the connection between theology and everyday life, I am not making any claims about its distinctiveness or importance. Appreciation of the importance of everyday life as a context for Christian reflection is being shown by others, some of whom will come into focus in the pages ahead. But so that my story will not stand alone, let me mention three others at this point.

*　　*　　*

The first is the highly respected and widely read author Frederick Buechner. A Presbyterian minister, Buechner many years ago realised that his particular calling lay as a writer rather than as pastor in a congregation. Since making that decision he has turned out a steady stream of both fiction and non-fiction. All novels raise the deeper issues in life, especially those relating to God and his ways in the world. His other works address aspects of the relationship between theology and fiction or attempt to do theology in a fresh and very accessible way.

In the last few years Buechner has written his autobiography. He sees a close connection between autobiography and theology, for the latter is only a more logical, abstract expresson of a person's concrete experience of what God has revealed to them. For himself, this experience of God has a decidedly everyday cast about it. As he says of his autobiography:

> More as a novelist than as a theologian, more concretely than abstractly, I determined to try to describe my own life as evocatively and candidly as I could in the hope that such glimmers of theological truth as I believe I had glimpsed in it

would shine through my description more or less on their own. It seemed to me then, and it seems to me still, that if God speaks to us at all in this world, if God speaks anywhere, it is into our personal lives that he speaks. Someone we love dies, say. Some unforeseen act of kindness or cruelty touches the heart or makes the blood run cold. We fail a friend, or a friend fails us, and we are appalled at the capacity we all of us have for estranging the very people in our lives we need the most. Or maybe nothing extraordinary happens at all — just one day following another, helter-skelter, in the manner of days. We sleep and dream. We wake. We work. We remember and forget. We have fun and are depressed. And into the thick of it, or out of the thick of it, at moments of even the most humdrum of our days, God speaks.[2]

This conviction of the link between knowing God and every-day events led Buechner earlier to write a book entitled *The Alphabet of Grace* which focussed on a single, ordinary day of his life. In the book, through describing the situations and events that made up the day — waking up, dressing, taking the children to school, working, and coming home again — he sought to suggest something of what he thought God was saying to him.

A second example is provided by Parker Palmer. Unlike Buechner, his background is in sociology rather than theology. Being a Quaker, he has never sought ordination. In his wonderfully stimulating and original book *The Company of Strangers: Christians and the Renewal of Public Life in America*, Palmer reveals aspects of his own pilgrimage. His journey has led him to become a member of a residential community. He has also had a close association with, indeed helped initiate, an institute and centre concerned to relate Christianity and life in the world. He has also been closely involved with the development of theological education for the wider Christian public.

---

2. F. Buechner, *The Sacred Journey*, 1982; *Now and then*, 1983; and *Alphabet of Grace*, 1970 — all Harper and Row

Although, as the title of his book suggests, he is dealing more with the public arena of life, he does not define this in the narrow terms of the political dimension. As he defines it, this arena covers more of what I have termed 'all the business of life' than the title of his book appears to suggest. For example, he identifies some of the places where public life comes to expression:

> The most likely place is the public street where strangers in pursuit of private interests meet each other... city parks, squares, sidewalk cafes, museums and galleries are also settings for the public life... Rallies, forums, hearings and debates (including those conducted by means of the public media) are settings in which the public interacts and becomes aware of itself... He also speaks of occasions 'where a street musician is playing, or at carnivals, festivals and fairs... The neighbourhood is another important setting for public life. Voluntary associations are also settings in which strangers come together and receive training... So the settings in which public life happens are many and diverse.[3]

Here, then, is another's story and approach to some of the same issues, forcefully and imaginatively argued, with wide-ranging implications for Christian thought and behaviour. Although his book is particularly designed for the American scene, it has much to say to people in other advanced industrial societies.

A third example of someone wrestling with the relevance of everyday experience for our understanding of God and obedience to him is Charles Cummings. His situation is very different to that of either Buechner or Palmer. In one sense he seems to be removed from many of the exigencies of life that most people face, for Cummings belongs to a Catholic order, one that operates according to quite stringent disciplines. But we have learned from Thomas Merton that the

3. Parker J. Palmer, *The Company of Strangers: Christians and the Renewal of Public Life in America*, Crossroads, 1981

contemplative life can sometimes put a person into closer contact with certain realities of everyday life than a more activist approach, precisely because the contemplative really does engage with those realities rather than simply hurrying through them.

This is the case with Charles Cummings who has undertaken advanced study in the area of spiritual formation and has committed himself to exploring contemporary modes of spiritual deepening for the benefit of ordinary Christians. In particular, drawing on a quarter of a century of reflection on ordinary aspects of life, he seeks to show others how much relating to and following God is interwoven with the texture of the simplest daily activities. As he says:

> We may live in extraordinary times, but most of us spend the greater part of our existence doing quite ordinary things. Our simple, everyday experiences can, however, put us in touch with the deepest mystery of life... Unfortunately the sameness and repetition of everyday activities can numb our awareness to the power. We get nothing out of the ordinary, and so conclude that nothing of value is there. Instead we seek extraordinary experiences and the special techniques that might induce such states. We put religious experience too easily into the category of the unusual, and never expect to find God in the usual things we do. The rich, spiritual dimension of our ordinary activities is thus lost to us.[4]

In his book *The Mystery of the Ordinary*, Cummings looks at such mundane activities as hearing, seeing, walking, resting, standing and eating, suggesting ways in which God is present in or can be served through them. Whereas Buechner concentrates on the relevance of the commonplace for one's life journey or vocation, and Palmer for our public life and responsibilities, Cummings attends more to its sig-

---

4. Charles Cummings, *The Mystery of the Ordinary*, Harper and Row, 1982

nificance for our understanding of God and the transformation of our character.

So, then, just as there are various stories to be told from the side of ordinary Christians about the everyday issues that confront them, so there are other stories from the side of those who are seeking to bring theological insight into touch with the ongoing business of life.

How this book came about

I have made it clear, I hope, that this book is not just an intellectual exercise, but has arisen out of increasing practical involvement in the issues it raises. It is not enough to think about the problem and then throw out a few untried suggestions. We have too much of this already in Christian circles and it has not overcome much of our present irrelevance. I realise that in some Christian circles there is too much doing and not enough thinking. That creates its own set of problems, many of which distract us from the real work God wishes us to do. Here I wish merely to emphasise the need for a closer and reciprocal connection between study and activity, thinking and doing, writing and experimenting.

This book did not only arise out of practical involvement in the area under discussion. It was stimulated by meeting with people from a number of Christian organisations in my own city who are seeking to help Christians relate their faith to their everyday lives. For me it has been essentially a practical exercise.

If you are a professional theologian or Christian educationalist, I have sought to address your concerns at points in the book. But throughout I have had a broader audience in view. If you are wanting to integrate your beliefs with your everyday life in a thoughtful way, then I am writing for you as well. I even have an eye on those of you who may not be convinced about Christianity, but have become aware that there is a spiritual dimension to life and that this should have a practical bearing upon your life.

But right at this point I have a difficulty. Such is the gap between theologians on the one hand and thoughtful Christians on the other, let alone those who are not yet persuaded to become Christians, that it is hard to know how to speak to all three groups at the same time. For example, a friend who has been manager of several Christian and general bookshops told me that the appearance of the word 'theology' in the title would be 'the kiss of death' so far as marketing the book generally was concerned. But for a professional theologian or theological student, it is the very presence of the word 'theology' that is likely to attract attention. The word 'theology' is just one example of the problem of writing for a diverse audience. On the whole these groups have different starting points, use different language and argue in different ways.

But I have taken the plunge, hoping there will be readers from all three groups at the other end of the page. I take heart from the comments of two writers who have attempted to bridge this gap. The successful German theological communicator, Helmut Thielicke, said that when he wished to draw people into his church in Hamburg who were not there at present, he prepared addresses for and spoke to them even though he knew they would not initially turn up. Only so would they actually begin to come! C.S. Lewis also once observed that it was far easier to write for a specialist audience than for a broader one, but that there was a greater need to write for the latter. In so doing both groups would actually be catered for.

So then I have tried to keep technical terms and theological jargon to a minimum. Yet I have not been afraid to use such language where it gives more precision to the argument or is a convenient form of shorthand. On the whole I have avoided discussion of academic theological views and schools since these will be unfamiliar to many of you and would not warrant the extra space needed to explain them satisfactorily. But for those interested, the appendix contains a discussion of some representative works and movements.

Footnotes are also not too numerous, though here and there I have included some that point the way to helpful resources.

I would not want you to begin this book with false expectations. If you come to it uncertain about the extent to which there is a divorce between Christian thinking and all the business of life,but open to find out to what extent this exists, you will find ample to help you work this out. I have gone into some detail about the size and character of this gap and have discussed why it exists and who is chiefly to blame. You will also find a strong challenge to you to do something to overcome it. But I have not attempted to present a complete set of arguments or testimonies to undergird my case.

If, on the other hand, you are only too well aware of the gap between your faith and your everyday life, and desperately want to close that gap, this book will not do it all for you. This is not because I have failed to wrestle enough with the problem nor because I have failed to give practical suggestions as to what you might do. It does not close the gap because you are the only ones who can do so. I have outlined the range of issues which require attention and identified the obstacles which must be overcome. I will point you to ways in which you could begin to bridge the gap and to resources which will help you along the way. More than that I cannot do. Otherwise I take too much of the privilege and responsibility for what needs to be done out of your hands.

Finally, I also want to allay in advance fears that some people express about too great a concentration upon everyday aspects of life, feeling perhaps that it diverts attention from the main task of commending the gospel to the people around us. One of the continuing threads throughout this book is the relationship between practical obedience and evangelistic concern. In one sense, the book is an extended commentary on the biblical injunction not to be conformed to this world but to present our whole selves as living sacrifices to God. In another sense it fleshes out the notion that verbal presentation of the gospel is inadequate unless it is framed within what is commonly referred to as lifestyle evangelism.

In addition, the book suggests that it is disturbing that we provoke so little interest in and so few questions about the gospel.

It also suggests that the reason why much preaching and teaching fails to strike home is because it does not begin from or connect up with real-life situations and dilemmas that everyone faces. As Jacques Ellul says:

> I know very well that people will say: 'Isn't simple preaching enough?' In reality the so-called confidence in the 'efficacy of the word of God' betrays a lack of charity towards man and an indifference to their actual situation; to some extent it is a 'spirituality' which is not in accordance with the mind of Christ.
>
> The Bible always shows us God laying hold of man in his practical situation; in the setting of his life, enabling him to act with the means of his own time, in the midst of the problems of his own day. But to want to copy the methods of Irenaeus or of Calvin means that we are both mistaken and unfaithful... our own day presents very complicated problems; our organisation is more complex than that of past centuries; and the same is true of questions which challenge the Christian faith and conscience... in the heart of this conflict, the word can be proclaimed but nowhere else.
>
> When we have really understood the actual plight of our contemporaries, when we have heard their cry of anguish, when we have understood why they won't have anything to do with our 'disembodied gospel', when we have shared their sufferings, both physical and spiritual, in their despair and desolation, when we have become one with the people of our own nation... as Moses and Jeremiah were one with their own people, as Jesus identified himself with the wandering crowds, 'sheep without a shepherd,' *then* we shall be able to proclaim the word of God — but not till then![5]

---

5. J. Ellul, *The Presence of the Kingdom*, SCM, 1951, pp.139-140

Unless we can do something about the pressures people live with today, they will be more closed to the gospel than they need be. In all these and other ways there is a close link between the concerns of this book and the fundamental place of evangelism.

2

The credibility gap

I NEED TO SAY A WORD ABOUT some of the terms that I am using continually throughout this book. In discussing the gap that so often exists between our basic system of beliefs and the general business of life, I have suggested the need for what I have called a 'theology of everyday life'. In order to avoid possible confusion, I wish to look at the way in which these words are being used.

The meaning of the key terms
1. What exactly is theology?
During a visit some months ago, a pastor from one of the churches in my home city commented: 'Of course mine is a fairly typical congregation — not interested in theology or anything like that.' He was right. Most Christians do not view theology in a positive light. The word suggests something rather esoteric. It has an other-worldly ring about it. As for people outside the church, long ago I found that describing myself as a theologian was usually the end of the conversation. Either they changed the topic or moved on hurriedly to someone else in the room. Someone who introduced himself as an astrologist would probably get a better hearing.

What about people who have no trouble with the word? What does the word *theology* mean to them? Normally it refers to the activity of exploring and organising Christian beliefs in a systematic way. This is carried out by a group of specialists who have high academic qualifications in the area.

You normally find theology in learned books and articles, in seminaries and religious studies departments, in professional conferences and seminars. But this usage is too narrow. Theology is — or ought to be — a much wider enterprise. In fact, part of the problem the average person has with theology stems from the fact that it seems to exist in a specialist world of its own.

But how broadly should we understand it? Occasionally you will hear someone suggest that it refers to any attitude towards Christianity, however rudimentary or unsystematic that may be. Just as people talk about everyone having some 'philosophy of life', so all Christians necessarily have a theology of some kind. This theology is made up of knowledge derived from sermons or conferences, personal reading and study groups, tapes or articles.

Now undoubtedly everyone does have views about life as well as values they live by. Christians also have some notion of what they believe in and how they should conduct themselves. But it is not very helpful to describe the first as a philosophy and the second as a theology of life unless a person reflects on and organises their beliefs in some degree. The seeds of a theology may exist prior to someone doing this, but nothing more.

In order for you to have a theology, therefore, you must give some thought to what you believe and develop some coherence in your understanding. Not everyone does this, not even those who engage in personal or group Bible-study. Such study may be so devotional in orientation that very little genuine thinking takes place. Or thinking may take place within so rigid a doctrinal framework that people do not have the freedom to develop their own understanding of God and his ways. I do not mean that devotional concern and strong convictions are incompatible with theology. It is just that in themselves these are not enough to constitute it. Nor am I saying that only those with formal education can have a theology. All you need is a willingness to think about truth and organise your conclusions. This is by no means confined to nor is it guaranteed by possession of an academic degree.

What then about learning that takes place through Christian education programmes in local churches, para-church groups or denominational colleges? Here we are on firmer ground. These tend to invite more serious discussion and to be more highly focussed. Occasionally they lack sufficient depth to take people very far. Sometimes they are too piecemeal in their approach. But at their best they provide a pathway to a maturer and more ordered understanding. For that reason it is a pity that such programmes tend to be described as Christian rather than theological education. This is somewhat of a put-down, for it reserves theological education for those who go to 'academic' Christian institutions or read 'serious' religious books.

Between this type of theological learning and the most sophisticated post-graduate forms, there are many intermediate levels, as there are between so-called Christian education programmes and personal or group Bible-study. Also it would be a mistake to think that theology only had to do with the Bible or with lectures and libraries. Theology comes from the wisdom you distil through quiet and disciplined reflection on the world God has created or upon the nature of life in general. The quest for understanding of the experience of God in your life and the desire to integrate this with other things you have learned also leads to theological understanding. So too does conversation with God, where this involves regular and sustained meditation on who he is and what he asks. In fact, any of these can be more genuinely theological than certain kinds of academic study of theology. Though the latter may focus on some aspect of Christianity in a concentrated way, the thinking that goes on may take place at a purely historical or philosophical level. Even study of the Bible or of systematic theology in such a setting can be a purely intellectual exercise. There is little vital personal involvement through the subject matter with God himself and little concern to practice what is understood.

When I use the word 'theology' in this book, then, I am

referring to any endeavour on the part of Christians to think through and set in order their beliefs, with the intention of drawing closer to God and reflecting more of his character in their lives. Where I have the more sophisticated type of theology in mind, I shall qualify the term by words such as 'professional' or 'academic'. In doing this I am not, by means of an inverse snobbery, dismissing its value. High-level theology has its place. It has a real contribution to make to understanding everyday life from a Christian point of view. But this requires changes in the prevailing attitudes and models which govern so much of it. As for theology in the broader sense, sometimes I have used synonyms such as 'thinking Christianly', 'developing a Christian perspective' or 'gaining a Christian understanding'. I have done this to avoid overuse of the word 'theology', especially since it may still be a barrier to some of you reading this book.

2. What makes up everyday life?

The term *everyday life* seems clear enough but it is not as obvious in meaning as it appears. This is a shorthand way of talking about what the title of this book refers to as 'all the business of life'. In general by *everyday life* I mean the regular situations we find ourselves in throughout the day or week, the ongoing responsibilities we have or activities we engage in, the issues that regularly claim our attention, the most insistent pressures that we feel, the things that we commonly think and talk about, the desires, values and beliefs that most shape our lives. I shall spell these out in more detail in the following chapter.

Obviously not everyone would describe what makes up their everyday life in identical terms: it is a complex and many-sided affair, varying according to factors such as gender, class and nationality. As a result they look at life differently, feel differently about even the same things and respond differently to similar circumstances. For example, men and women do not always approach people, issues or situations in the same way. In a similar fashion, the socioeconomic level at which you live tends to affect the way you view the world and react to it. This is more noticeable when we consider ethnic differences where a great deal of humour and tragedy has resulted from the clashing perceptions of people who belong to different ethnic groups. Other differences such as how old we are, where we live, how much formal education we have had and whether we are handicapped or not, alter our understanding and experience of everyday life.

So when I use the phrase *everyday life* I am talking about a multiple reality and to do it justice we need a variety of attempts to think Christianly or theologise about it. These would have different groups as their focus and be written in a different style. For the style needs to match the audience for which it is intended. While there would be a number of common threads between classes, each would also have distinctive elements. I am writing as a male, middle-class Anglo-Saxon living in a medium-sized Australian city. Though I have made a genuine attempt to think beyond this and enter into others' situations, my choice of concerns and the way I approach them will be partly affected by who, where and what I am.

How far have the issues of everyday life been addressed by professional theologians? Although various schools of thought have turned in its direction during the last thirty years, they have only explored some of its territory.

In the sixties we saw the emergence of what was called a *secular or political theology.* This attempted to draw our attention to the importance of what was happening in the world generally and to what we could do about it. Much emphasis was laid on the need for Christians to come to grips more positively with the secular nature of modern society and to become politically involved in making it a more human place in which to live. These movements generally looked at the world through a large telescope, identifying trends that we needed to be aware of or reminding us of measures we could take to influence our society. This was helpful, even if they did overplay the extent to which our society is really secular and the amount that can be achieved through the political process. But neither of these approaches brought into focus our day-to-day concerns and activities in a close-up way.

Over the last decade and a half there has also been considerable interest in developing a *contextual or indigenous theology*. Too often in the past professional theologians have ignored the concrete situation in which they worked and the particular society of which they were a part. For example, I cannot remember any serious attention being given in my theological education to the fact that I would be ministering in a large city. Nor to the fact that both myself and the people around me had been shaped by the particular history and geography associated with being Australian. It was as if place or nationality had no bearing whatever on what people were like or on how I might bring the gospel to them. But now some Christian thinkers have begun to identify what is distinctive about life in our own country and to discuss how living in it affects us. There are materials here relevant to a theology of everyday life, particularly in connection with the basic values and popular rites of many Australians. But this material touches on only certain groups in our society. It has, for example, been very male-orientated, and even so affects only certain aspects of their everyday lives.

In recent years we have seen a renewed interest in *personal and social ethics*. Some of the work that has been done in this area is fairly theoretical. Some of it has taken up personal moral dilemmas that many people, including Christians, face, such as divorce and remarriage. But a number of issues that concern these writers — abortion or euthanasia, for example — are not regular problems for any individual, though none the less important for that. Many of the broader social dilemmas these writers address — unemployment or the nuclear threat, for instance — do impinge upon our lives in a real way and form the context in which we live.

Yet these writers do not always give us much guidance as to what we can do at a practical level about these and other problems. This guidance has been given most fully in the area of lifestyle, though it is not always professional theologians who have the most helpful things to say. In any case, life is more than a series of moral dilemmas and only partly covered through an ethics-orientated approach.

In recent years we have heard increasing reference to the need for a *lay and a liberation theology*. Lay theology has sought to emphasise the importance of every Christian both in the church and in the world and the need for each person to fashion a thoughtful Christian perspective on every activity. Liberation theology has insisted that theological work begin with the concerns of the people rather than intellectual problems and has begun to pioneer ways of doing this. At their best these theological movements come closest to bringing theology down-to-earth, even if they are not fully aware of what is involved in this. At their worst they are too church- or work-orientated on the one hand or too uncritically purely ideological and politicised on the other.[1]

There has also been renewed interest in *pastoral and practical theology*. Pastoral theology deals with such matters as rites of passage and different life stages as well as some of the dilemmas of personal and family life. The theological appraisal of these enters the sphere of everyday life in a significant way, but only touches certain aspects of it. In the past, practical theology has concentrated on various dimensions of ordained ministry such as preaching, liturgy, religious education and church management. Now it is being widened to include the vocation of all Christians, in the world as well as in the church. So viewed, this also overlaps with a theology of everyday life, but to date the emphasis has fallen upon an expanded approach to clerical training with a view to empowering ordinary Christians to fulfil their ministry, or upon an expansive concern with social justice and global issues. In both, the seminary remains central.

---

1. N. Pittenger, *The Ministry of All Christians: A theology of lay ministry*, Morehouse-Barlow, 1983

The gap between belief and daily life

In the remainder of this chapter I would like to formulate ten theses. These have their basis in the experiences of a wide range of people who have corroborated or extended my own conclusions about the relationship between belief and all the business of life. Some of these people I have met, corresponded with and engaged in discussion. Others are only known to me through their writings. In each of the statements that follow I have drawn on the experience of one of these people. The first five of these theses will explore the gap many of us perceive between our faith and our everyday lives. All I am doing in this section is building on what is common knowledge to those seeking to develop an integrated Christian life. The final five of these will examine the gap that exists between theology as it is written and taught today and everyday life. Less has been written about this and the gap is far wider than most imagine.

1. *Few of us apply or know how to apply our belief*
   to our work, or lack of work.

Ten years ago a book appeared entitled *Christianity and Real Life*, written by the sales manager for a major overseas steel corporation. I came across the book a couple of years later and it struck deep chords in my own mind. For here was a thinking Christian, speaking from the heart of the modern workplace, who wrote in an anguished way about the credibility gap he felt in his own life. In the preface to the book, William Diehl wrote:

> This book is about two gaps. The first gap is the one which is present in my life and in the lives of thousands of dedicated laypeople. It is the gap between our Sunday faith and our weekday world.
>
> The second gap is the one... between what the church proclaims as the role of Christian laypersons in the world and what the church actually does to support that role.
>
> The two gaps are closely interrelated.[2]

---

2. W. Diehl, *Christianity and Real Life*, Fortress, 1976, p.v.

I will say more about the second of these gaps later. Here I simply wish to underline the distance Diehl was aware of between his religious beliefs and his responsibilities at work.

Many other Christians are also conscious of this gap. Some of you may be troubled by the pressures you are under at work. Others may feel frustrated because of the kind of work you have to do. Or you may be concerned about the quality of the decisions you have to make, the values of the place you work for, the structures within which you carry out your job or the goals of the institution in which you serve. In his book Diehl only concerns himself with work of this kind, that is with paid employment. But there are many other kinds of work and they also raise questions for those undertaking them.

Work may take the form of housework, study, voluntary help or vocational training, as well as paid employment. Work needs to be understood more widely than it is in most discussions of a 'lay theology'. Such discussions leave too many people out of account and, incidentally, give these the impression that they do not make much of a contribution. Interpreting it in its broadest sense, work occupies more of our time than any other activity. This gives it a special significance in our lives.

Despite a gradual lowering of statutory and actual working hours, certain groups in our society are now working longer than ever before. It's now very common to find such people regularly bringing home work in the evenings or over the weekend. Despite the proliferation of labour-saving devices, the increased size of homes and yards today and the increased expectations about cleanliness and presentation have resulted in little reduction in the number of hours spent on domestic work. There has also been a fairly steady rise in the amount of time young people give to their education or training. In addition to this time factor, many women are confused about the status and value of the work involved in raising a family and looking after a home. Some students are uncertain about the vocational or personal value of the studies they have to undertake. And in the official workforce itself, more and more people appear to be experiencing a mid-life crisis.

We also have the problem of long-term or endemic unemployment to worry about. Jobs are now very much harder to get. Educational qualifications do not guarantee employment any more, though they certainly help. If you are older you have more chance, but middle-aged people as well as the young are now victims of our economic misfortunes. Many more of you will be out of work in the future or only able to get part-time jobs. Our economy is on a continuing downturn and there is no reversal in sight.

This situation is raising broader questions about the nature, significance and character of work. But these are already real issues for some people. Some of you are facing a threat to your job, if not right now then at some point down the road. Some of you have a job, but it is not the one you trained for or would prefer to have. You may even have formal theological qualifications or be a clergyman and experience this. Some of you are wondering whether you made the right choice in the first place and whether you should now head in a new direction. If you are in any of these situations, how well have you been able to make sense Christianly of what is happening to you?

2. *We make only minimal connections between our faith
and our spare time activities.*

What people do in their spare time varies in importance from one person to the next. For some it is secondary to their main concerns. For others it is central to their life. Recently, I was talking to a friend about this. In the course of our conversation he told me about a young married woman who attended his church. This woman had discovered within herself a deep interest in art. She had begun to attend classes to learn more about it and to develop her creative skills. While she gave the major part of her time to bringing up her small family, whatever time was left over she devoted to her new-found interest. This interest had helped overcome her feeling of simply being an extension of her husband and children. It had enriched and given added meaning to her life.

It was bringing out gifts within her that she never knew she possessed. Yet she was having difficulty integrating it with her Christianity. She found it hard to talk to people about what she was doing for no one seemed to be able to enter into it. She knew of no other models for bringing together these two aspects of her life. The world of other Christians and the world of her art interests never seemed to meet. So much so that she admitted to my friend that when she went to church on Sundays 'so narrow is the scope of what I can talk about and what happens that I feel I have to leave half of myself behind at home.'

Not everyone would place as much importance on their spare time activities as this young woman. But that does not mean that those activities are insignificant either for ourselves or for God. Of course some people do not have much spare time anyway. Sometimes economic necessities in low income families force one or more members of a family to take on two jobs to 'moonlight'. The long distances some people have to travel to get work places pressure upon their time and occasionally even breaks a family up. The person bringing up children in a single-parent family faces extra demands that sometimes leave them little time for leisure. Women with a number of young children often find little rest from early morning to well on in the evening. Young couples trying to buy a home are both under pressure these days to work for some years in order to save a deposit. In such cases the problem is how to create sufficient spare time for relaxation and refreshment. However, while many of us have less spare time than we realise — why else would we be complaining so much about how little time we have? — on average most of us can devote up to 10% of our time to freely-chosen activities. We use this time in different ways and many are finding it difficult to judge how to use this time in the most fitting way.

Part of the problem is due to the feeling that these days many spare time activities involve harder work than our weekday jobs. Some are becoming aware that it is better to keep up the addictive pace of work in their spare time rather than face the painful withdrawal symptoms they would have if they really relaxed. On the other hand, some are also becoming aware that it is easy to reduce leisure pursuits merely into an escape from work or compensation for work. How can we honour the spirit of the fourth commandment in our kind of society and turn our spare time activities into the fulfilment of our work, an end in themselves, with their own distinctive rhythms and rewards?

But many of us feel guilty about taking time off to do 'nothing much' when we have spare time, even though we know it is one of the things God has commanded. Generally we find it difficult to establish a balance between work and leisure. We are also unsure how to proportion leisure and church-related activities. Yet apart from hesitating to play in games on Sundays and having a sense that sport is about fair play, few of us have any idea about how we might develop a Christian perspective on our leisure.

3. *We have little sense of a Christian approach to*
   routine or monotonous activities.

Every so often I come across people who feel bound and frustrated by their circumstances. Mostly this is a woman whose major time is spent at home with a growing family. As one such person said to me: 'Sometimes I feel that I'm just stuck in the house, tied to the kitchen sink and washing machine. All I seem to do is clear up after the kids — just one thing after another. I spend half the evening catching up on chores I haven't been able to do during the day. I hardly ever open a book or if I do I get only part of the way through it. My husband does what he can when he's around. He's very helpful really. But some days I get so frustrated that I could bang my head against the wall until I drop.'

Some of you have probably felt this way! I know my own

wife did at one stage in her life. I even came close to it myself on one occasion when I had to look after everything at home for a period.

This situation could be paralleled in much large-scale factory work, in the pedestrian character of many low-level office jobs or in certain positions held down in shops and supermarkets. A particularly severe instance of this is the underpaid, high-pressured work that goes on in many textile industries, much of which exploits the services of migrant women who find it difficult to get other employment. But not all our routine situations are this extreme or as depressing as this example. If you work at home you probably find certain things that you do or certain times of the day more congenial than others. If you are in paid employment, there are many things you do before you start work at nine o'clock in the morning, during your lunch hour and after five o'clock in the evening which have to be done but are not necessarily frustrating. In both cases there are also activities you engage in on weekends and on holidays, apart from leisure pursuits.

These are not all or always draining, though sometimes they can become rather monotonous. Most of our time goes simply on personal maintenance. Sleeping, as we noted earlier, takes up about a third of our time, while washing, dressing, grooming and eating occupy another 10% of our time over our total life-span. If you are employed, when you add personal maintenance to your domestic chores, this amounts to approximately the same amount of time you spend at work: around 15%. If you are mainly a homemaker, you spend only marginally less time on these two activities than those in paid employment. Then there is the time spent in shopping, chauffering children, running errands and attending meetings: about 5% of our time overall is spent on travelling.

Quite apart from these activities and the daily round of domestic chores, both work and leisure can contain a routine element. For example, if you are employed, much of what you do in the early stages of your career can be fairly monotonous. So too if you are still at school or attending a college or university. The apparent meaninglessness of so much routine activity lies at the root of many personal problems. Yet, apart from memories of the example of Brother Lawrence at the kitchen sink and admonitions about learning to be content in every situation, how are we able to tie in our routine activities with the obligation to place the kingdom of God first in our lives? Some Christians are deeply aware of this gap. But since they cannot remain too long in it, frequently they look for an escape into some 'Christian' work that has more apparent meaning or they resign themselves to 'wasting' much of their time each day on humdrum matters. Yet others will not settle for this and persist in seeking a better alternative.

4. *Our everyday attitudes are partly shaped by*
   the dominant values of our society.

A couple of years ago a nationwide survey was carried out to discover the dominant values of Australian people. The results of this survey are disturbing in some respects. While some Christian groups, especially those in more conservative churches, do think and act differently to the majority of people, the general attitudes and priorities of most church-goers are not very different from others. In some respects even the more distinctive Christian groups are not all that dissimilar to the population at large. They do exhibit a different attitude on some personal and social moral issues, but this is less noticeable in some of their basic goals and values.[3]

   Comparisons with other Western countries suggest that the attitudes and priorities of Christians within them are not dissimilar. The same social forces, norms and pressures affect us all and many of these operate in hidden and pervasive ways which are difficult to detect and resist. Many Christians do have a strong sense of their fundamental

---

3. In particular see the monograph by G. Bouma and Beverley Dixon, *The Religious Factor in Australian Life*, MARC — World Vision, Zadok, 1986

beliefs and standards, but find it difficult to know exactly how these apply to the varied and complex situations that confront them. Most of us have an innate suspicion of materialistic attitudes, of becoming worldly and of a relaxed approach to morals. But it is hard to remain unaffected by the acquisitive impulse, to discern the subtle forms which worldliness takes or to know how to deal with grey rather than black-and-white moral situations.

This is why a gap so often opens up between the private profession of faith and its public performance. This does not necessarily make Christians hypocrites in the sense in which that term is used today, for mostly they want to avoid living in a way that is self-contradictory. But it does make Christians hypocrites in the biblical sense of the word. That is, they say one thing but without realising it do another. Christians are unaware how much they are influenced by the basic assumptions, such as individualism, on which our society rests, or by its ideological attitudes, such as increasingly having a consumer attitude, even towards the church and God.

Some Christians sense this and are trying to do something about it. They want to identify their underlying beliefs and values and find out how consonant they are with Christ's teaching. They want to apply that teaching to the tangled web of pressures, aspirations, dilemmas, concerns and situations that daily come their way. But, as they are discovering, this is not easy. Quite apart from anything else, there is so much to think through, decide on and do something about. What matters should have priority and what do they do about those matters that for the time being they have to leave to one side? Even with the help of others it is a slow, often confusing and sometimes painful process.

5. *Many of our spiritual difficulties stem from the daily pressures we experience.*

Some time ago I received an interesting letter from a regional denominational head. This came as a response to a short article I had written on how few Christians bought or read books of a religious nature. In the article I talked about the poor quality and especially the unreality of so much Christian literature. Taking up what I said about the irrelevance of so much Christian literature to the concerns of the average Christian, the Bishop asked how much research had been done on the day-to-day problems that the majority of Christians face. He had begun to see the need for this, he said, as the result of a recent experience in his Diocese:

> Recently I conducted a Mission in a nearby country town. Before I conducted the Mission I asked each member of the Parish Council to answer a question, and the question I put was, 'What is it in your Christian experience that most deters you from Christian belief or Christian behaviour? In other words, what is the single element that makes it most difficult for you to believe and behave in a Christian manner?' I asked each member of the Parish Council to do that exercise privately and not to confer with other members of the Council. I then collected the results and was astonished to find that more than half of them said that the one thing that most prevented them from believing and behaving as a Christian was the nature of society itself. The most common element that set up this hurdle was the pressures they found in society. I had anticipated getting answers like how difficult it was to understand or read the Bible, or how unreal it seemed to be saying prayers, or other answers of a semi-religious nature. For the purposes of that Mission I changed the whole teaching and first of all tried to describe modern society and then to suggest some Christian answers.

Of course, some people — both within the church and outside it — do have genuine intellectual or moral problems with Christianity. However, most do not, even when they cast their questions in the form of intellectual and moral objections. Some people's difficulties with Christianity do arise from a lack of biblical knowledge or an inadequate devotional life. But often it is external factors which make it hard for people to clear time to read the Bible and pray, not some inner weakness. Even those who manage to overcome these difficulties sometimes find it hard to relate what they believe and what they read in the Bible to their daily responsibilities. When they go to church they may find it difficult to relate the sermon and prayers to what they are involved in during the remainder of the week.

This gap between religious convictions and ordinary activities is due to a number of factors. For example, if in the office or factory where people work they are only able to refer to God occasionally, it is easy for them to begin thinking and talking less about God in general. As well, since they need a pragmatic outlook to function well on the job, this slowly begins to affect the way they approach non-work areas of life, even what goes on in their church or spiritual life. Alternatively, a deadening or impersonal job can in the long term have a dulling effect upon people's personality, outlook and relations in general, carrying over into the spiritual dimension as well. This is part of the reason why so many blue collar workers have been alienated in the past from Christianity and are still less attracted to it today.

Busyness and the need to work late also start to impinge upon the quality of their relating to God and others. These are some of the reasons why so many Christians are reticent about their faith at work. (It also explains why some become hyper-spiritual, compensating for the lack of a religious dimension in their work by taking a charismatic overdose elsewhere.) Ministers frequently trace this gap to a lack of singlemindedness towards Christ. But it is not yielding to obvious temptations from the world that is always the problem. It is the discordance people feel between the world they inhabit most of the week and the world of churchgoing and religious practices.

6. *Our everyday concerns do not receive much attention in the church.*

Three years ago my wife and I were leading a mission in a

mainline church in the South Island of New Zealand. This ran over three weeks and included a mixture of sermons, addresses, seminars, dialogues and conversations. We decided to focus the mission on the theme 'Getting in Touch', looking in turn at how to establish contact with oneself, others and God. The mission began with an opening service at which I preached on the way busyness resulted in our losing touch with all of these. After the service I was approached by a middle-aged businessman who said that he did not go to church very often. 'When my wife reminded me that the mission was starting this morning,' he said, 'I tossed up whether I would bother coming or not. I thought to myself "You'll only have to sit through another sermon, so what's the point?" I almost didn't come. But when you spoke, I didn't hear a sermon at all. Instead I heard someone talking about what was actually going on in my own life.'

His reaction is most revealing. For him, and I suspect many others, a sermon by definition did not bear any relation to everyday life. It was something other-worldly, in the worst rather than best sense of the term. Helmut Thielicke writes about this problem in his book, *The Trouble with the Church*:

> The real crisis in preaching under which we are suffering [is] a modern variant of Docetism... when a sermon does not 'hit home', the reason need by no means lie in the fact that it contained no examples from life nor that it was too theoretical... it may lie in the fact that the preacher is speaking on the basis of a Docetic view of human beings and that the person of whom he is speaking and whom he is addressing does not appear in the sermon at all. Then the very hearers who are troubled by real situational problems feel that they have been bypassed. And perhaps the only ones who listen are those who are largely removed from the worldly situation.[4]

---

4. H. Thielicke. *The Trouble with the Church*, Baker, 1965, p.76

This is why, as Thielicke goes on to mention, the majority of Christians making a vital contribution today are not attending such services of worship. But what is true of sermons is true of church activities in general. To quote William Diehl again:

> ... In the almost thirty years of my professional career, my church has never once suggested that there be any type of accounting of my on-the-job ministry to others. My church has never once offered to improve those skills which could make me a better minister, nor has it ever asked if I needed any kind of support in what I was doing. There has never been an enquiry into the types of ethical decisions I must face, or whether I seek to communicate the faith to my co-workers. I have never been in a congregation where there was any type of public affirmation of a ministry in my career. In short, I must conclude that my church really doesn't have the least interest whether or how I minister in my daily work.[5]

Most Bible-studies are of little help here. They tend to concentrate on the exposition of biblical books or on the discussion of theological themes. Obviously these are basic concerns, but why is so little attention paid to the proverbial passages in the Bible or to the lives of some of the ordinary figures who feature in it? Doctrinal topics or broader social and political questions, perfectly valid in themselves, tend to squeeze out more everyday concerns in study groups. Even work-based Bible-studies and study groups rarely address the specific questions, dilemmas, pressures and aspirations that arise in the employment situation. In fact, the concentration upon pure Bible-study in some of these groups is often an escape from grappling with the real issues of life.

---

5. W. Diehl, op.cit., pp.v-vi

7. *Only occasionally do theological institutions*
address everyday life issues.

Several years ago I attended the annual conference of the
American Association for the Study of Religion and the
Society of Biblical Literature for the first time. This was held
in Dallas just before Christmas. I have attended many theological conferences in my time, but this was a new
experience for me. Dallas itself was very different to any
other American city I had visited. The conference was also
noticeably different. Its setting (in a luxurious hotel), its size
(around two thousand members), its range (some 800 papers
delivered over four days) and its atmosphere (purely professional) were all unfamiliar to me. Everyone attending had
received a thick, book-length manual setting out the arrange-
ments for the conference and abstracts of papers. It occurred
to me that it would be interesting to read through these to
see how many of the papers or main addresses took an issue
of everyday concern as a starting point, dealt centrally with
such a concern or contained implications in this direction. I
could count the number which did this on two hands.

While I have no difficulty with scholars working on highly
technical or even abstruse subjects, there was an imbalance
here which seemed out of all proportion. Of course, some
professional theologians do write books or articles on down-
to-earth matters to Christians. Some of these writings are
also addressed to a general audience. Topics treated in this
way include spirituality, personal relationships, the rites of
passage, current moral and social problems. But few academic theologians address the daily struggles, tensions and
situations that the majority of us, and even the majority of
them, face. In their writings, says Helmut Thielicke:

> we find men living on esoteric problems which crop up in the-
> ologians' conversations among themselves... or they get
> mired down in methodological considerations and disappear
> in the smoke of hermeneutics.[6]

---

6. H. Thielicke, op.cit., p.81

The appearance of that last word, hermeneutics — the science or art of interpretation — in a book by one of the best theological communicators this century, is enough to make most people run for cover.

The average Christian — and even the professional theologian — looking for help in an area of practical concern, is more likely to find it in books by non-scholarly authors. A number of these books have good things to say. In some of them there is more contemporary and theological awareness than in the work of many formally-trained theologians. Unfortunately, however, a large proportion of non-scholarly Christian books are superficial and misleading. Their grasp of concrete issues is insufficiently informed and their proposals for dealing with them too simplistic. I am not necessarily blaming them for this, for they too are victims of the gap between professional theology and the average Christian that I am discussing. It is certainly the shelves containing these books that attract potential buyers rather than the bays filled with contemporary theology.

8. *When addressed, everyday issues tend to*
   be approached too theoretically.
When I asked a public servant friend of mine who is a great reader some time ago why he read so few books by professional theologians, he said: 'Because almost none of the books of that kind I have read have that sense of reality I find in books by many of the non-Christian authors that I buy.' While his statement may be too extreme, it is not very wide of the mark. Many other Christians feel the same way.

As an inveterate reader myself, I used to find that the appearance of a new theological book by a celebrated writer or on an important topic held a great attraction. I would get hold of such a book as soon as I could and read it at the earliest opportunity. Often I would get through the book in a day or over a weekend, eager to find out whatever insights the author might have. Nowadays some of the magic has gone, partly because I choose to learn more from life at first-hand in a more holistic way than vicariously through another's writings, but partly because I have become increasingly disappointed with the books written by professional theologians, even about more practical concerns.

The trouble with the writings of so many academic theologians, even on matters of common concern, is that they are generally too abstract. They do not get close enough to the ordinary business of life to see it as it really is. Or, if they do get relatively close, they provide a 'still-life' portrait rather than a dynamic analysis. I can think of two reasons for this: sometimes they lack first-hand experience of the issue and are unable to speak about it in concrete terms; sometimes they do not have a sufficient knowledge of the social sciences or contemporary literature to supply a fully rounded description of it. The separation of many theologians from vital involvement in a congregation and the isolation of so much theology from other academic disciplines is part of the problem. But that is not all. We should remember, however, that in many respects academic theology is no worse off than what takes place in most other fields of knowledge.

So I do not want to lay all the blame on professional theologians or on theological institutions. And there are some real exceptions to what I am saying. But from the viewpoint of the average Christian, there is a real lack here. Many professional theologians look at the scene through long-range telescopes, observing some of the same everyday phenomena as others but frequently not seeing the whole picture. Moreover, as a consequence of the particular angle from which they are looking, certain objects have become magnified out of all proportion and others are blurred. This is why many people find that the writings of such theologians have an unreal atmosphere about them.

Even where formally-qualified theologians are not so out of touch with everyday concerns, another difficulty rears its head. A theological analysis of an issue may be clear and accurate, but what about the prescription for dealing with it? All too often this is very general. Only rarely will the theologian provide an operational model of what might be done and offer practical recommendations or examples drawn from first-hand experience. We are left up in the air, tantalised by a vision of what is possible, but without the means of realising it. The difficulty here is that most professional theologians are more engaged in talk than action. They are more inclined to interpret reality in the light of revelation rather than do much to actually change it.

9. *Only a minority of Christians read religious books or attend theological courses.*

Several years ago I was talking with the manager of a religious bookshop in one of our capital cities. He had just completed a piece of market research. To his surprise he found that even among churchgoers only a small percentage ever bought books from such a shop. Many more churchgoers bought or borrowed secular books than ever read religious ones. Despite the increase in people signing on for formal courses in theological instruction, the great majority of churchgoers have no interest in these. Some congregations do have a fair proportion of their members involved in study groups. A number of para-church organisations have also developed their own training programmes. In these groups and programmes more informal theological learning does go on. But most Christians never take part in such activities. Even those with tertiary qualifications rarely see the need for study, despite their willingness to attend seminars, workshops and conferences in their own professional field.

In his excellent book, *The Function of Theology*, Martin Thornton has something to say about this problem:

> It might be suggested that theology is the necessary theory behind religious practice, that it is the mainspring and directive behind practical Christian living. I believe that is, ultimately, the correct answer, but two overwhelming objections to it cannot be evaded. The first is that it does not appear to be so: were this the true answer, then why does not the modern interest in theology in all levels of society manifest

itself more obviously? The second objection is that if theology
is the necessary theory behind Christian practice, then those
most nearly concerned with its nurture and propagation do
not appear to think so: ministers of religion form a very small
proportion of the theology-reading public.[7]

Most churchgoers regard any kind of theological instruction,
formal or informal, as relevant only to a few. It is all right for
someone who is training for the ministry or who likes that
sort of thing, but they do not feel it has much to offer them.
If we look at those people who do read Christian literature
or attend theological institutions, we find that they do so
mostly for other reasons than developing Christian understanding of all the business of life. These people fall into two
groups. The first take up theology because they want to
understand more about the Bible, doctrine and church
history. This is a worthy aim. The difficulty is that few books
and courses of this kind speak the language or address the
interests of ordinary Christians. The second group want to
develop a Christian perspective on their discipline, occupation or some special area of concern. Few books and courses
emanating from theological institutions deal with these in a
direct and practical way. This means that even where some
Christians engage in reading and studying theology formally,
the gap between professional theology and everyday life
remains much as it was.

10. *Most churchgoers reject the idea of a gap between
their beliefs and their way of life.*
Some time ago I had the opportunity to visit most of the
capital cities in Australia and speak with Christian public servants about an attempt to bring a Christian perspective to
bear upon certain aspects of government administration. I
did this with a public servant from my home city who had

---

7. M.Thornton, *The Function of Theology*, Hodder and Stoughton, 1968,
   p.14

been involved in a working group addressing this issue. There was reasonable interest in the topic in most places we visited. But we were not prepared for the reception we received.

Nowhere were we able to assume the premise from which our working group had begun, which was that Christians should make a serious effort to integrate their faith with their work. In each place we visited a number of people took issue with this. They agreed that faith had something to do with their attitude and relationships at work, but not with the actual work itself or the institution in which the work was performed. At points they became quite hostile to any questioning of their position. Only a few people in each place affirmed the link between faith and work that we were advocating. The majority remained fairly quiet, unsure how to respond. Consequently we had to revise our approach to these meetings and begin with fundamentals.

Now if you ask a representative sample of churchgoers whether faith and life ought to be in harmony, they will answer with a resounding 'yes'. The rub comes when you put the question in a specific way, in relation to a particular aspect of work or area of responsibility. For example, if you are a homemaker and I ask you whether your religious convictions should influence the way you bring up your family and relate to your neighbours, you will probably nod your head in agreement.

But then if I ask you whether those convictions have as clear and direct an influence on the kind of house you have, area you live in and the means of commuting you use, you will probably pause to think. Unfortunately, we are unaware how much our decisions in these areas are moulded by broader social attitudes and have little distinctively Christian about them. Sometimes we are as affected by the attitudes and values of our society in these matters as much as people in a totalitarian society by their country's propaganda machine.

As the Christian educationalist Douglas Wingeier says:

It is too easy to lay all the blame for our ineptness in doing theology at the door of others. To be sure, the pluralism and individualism of our culture are bewildering, and the attitudes of dependency and dualism cultivated by the church are seductive. But in the final analysis, it is we who either resist or submit to those tendencies... We sense that to try to relate our faith to our daily life would require real effort and courage. We would have to take time to pray, reflect on our experience, and become more familiar with the Bible and Christian beliefs. And we would need to make our through-the-week behaviour more consistent with our Sunday affirmations. There could be some risk in this. So, for good reasons, we allow the weeks and years to go by, with the gap between our beliefs and our everyday experience remaining, or growing wider.[8]

We have to recognise this problem and confront it head on. Too much talk about Christian education and a theology of the people assumes that the majority of Christians are simply waiting for the right kinds of books and courses to come along for them to become enthusiastic readers and willing participants in courses that are offered. It would be nice if this were so. But it is just not the case. A minority will respond in that fashion. A number will say that they are interested, but when it comes to the point they will have other things to do. Many will not show much interest at all. Yet some of these are uneasy and can be encouraged to take the matter more seriously. For others, too much is at stake and the only way they will change their mind is by undergoing a radical conversion of their attitudes. But one thing is certain. As Wingeier says, deep down 'we know that if we are serious about being full-time Christians, we must make a habit of thinking theologically about our life. If we really want it to make sense again, we must begin doing theology in earnest.'[9]

8. D.E. Wingeier, *Working out Your Own Beliefs: A guide for doing your own theology*, Abingdon, 1980, pp.17-18
9. ibid.

Conclusion

In this chapter I have sought to do two things. First, I have endeavoured to show that some Christians are aware of a credibility gap between their beliefs and their everyday life. Second, I have suggested that professional theology and theological institutions have not done a great deal to overcome this gap. This results in a rather extraordinary situation. The matters which both occupy and preoccupy us the bulk of the time do not receive very much thoughtful Christian consideration. Academic theologians often concern themselves with only a limited range of human experience, leaving much largely unattended. Ordinary Christians often fear the cost involved in integrating their beliefs with their everyday lives.

This is not a happy situation. It leaves too many Christians as divided persons and too much of life out in the cold. It is time we broke out of this captivity and did justice to both belief and everyday life, and linked up these two aspects that God always intended should remain together.

3

The texture of daily life

ASPECTS OF ORDINARY LIFE I wish to consider are of
varying kinds. Some arise because of pressures placed upon
us by our society; others stem from routine activities in
which we are involved. Quite specific questions are raised in
the areas of work and leisure; and the central features of
modern life bring other issues to the fore. While what follows
is fairly detailed, it is not intended to be exhaustive. I am
aware that other matters could have been included.

I would like to stress that the following suggestions did not
come through simply sitting down and thinking them up.
They distil a considerable amount of personal and family
reflection on our own everyday activities. They have been
shaped by many hours of conversation with a wide range of
people willing to talk about their concerns. They are
influenced by experiences people have shared in home
churches to which we have belonged. Here and there I have
also come across books touching on the subject.

In drawing together the threads from these different
encounters, I am not wishing to impose upon others my conclusions concerning the issues to which a theology of everyday life should address itself: I am setting out the issues
which I see as important. What follows is more of a personal
agenda than a prescriptive list. Others' agendas may differ
from mine, though I would be surprised if they did not
contain many of the same elements. Certainly the actual
work of developing a Christian perspective on any one of

these issues, or any others that might be framed, can only begin with individuals' declarations of their own concerns.

Some general social pressures

Before I discuss a number of crucial social pressures, I suggest that you pause at this point and give some thought to these yourself. What are the major external pressures that surround and affect you? It may take you a little while to do this so do not hurry it. If you are tempted to bypass what I am suggesting here or hurry the process, you might ask yourself why you are inclined to do this.

All societies place pressures upon their members. These pressures are felt by some people more than others but no one entirely escapes their influence: they are too integral a part of life. I believe that the major pressures upon people in our own society are not peculiar to it: we share them, more or less, with all advanced industrial societies. The following are some of the main pressures we experience:

1. Busyness

It is not only the business of life that requires attention but the busyness that so often accompanies it. In this respect a new poverty has emerged in societies like our own over the last two centuries. It is a poverty of the affluent rather than the poor and a hidden poverty rather than one that is immediately recognisable. While a few groups have suffered as a result of this poverty before, it has never occurred on a mass scale as is happening now. We may not be poor economically as the majority of people are in the Two-thirds World, but we are poor in terms of time, whereas they tend to have an abundance of it. What we have gained in terms of material things, we have lost in terms of disposable time. This is especially true of those of us who are middle-class, tertiary-educated and in professional occupations. Yet it is also true of many migrant or working-class people on low incomes, single-parent families with slender support networks, self-employed people, and working wives who have to fit into others' schedules and patterns. And, because of church and other commitments, Christians are often worse off than others.

The fact of the matter is this: our days are overloaded with too many things to do and never enough time to do them all in. We are whisked along through a kaleidoscope of situations, appointments, activities and responsibilities for most of our waking hours. However much we try to get ahead, we never seem to catch up. The watch and the diary regulate our time and help us ration it out. We are enslaved to them and feel lost without them. Yet where does all this haste and regulation get us? Our bodies cannot take the pace and malfunction more often. Our nerves are stretched to breaking point and we suffer constitutional fatigue. We have little time for family, friends and neighbours. Life ends early for many — through heart attacks and premature death after retirement. Despite sermons on the need to 'redeem the time' and our attendance at 'time-management' seminars, most of us lack a genuine Christian perspective on our attitude to and use of time.[1]

2. Mobility

Every year about one in six Australians moves residence. A significant percentage of people rarely stay more than two or three years in the one place. Those who are unemployed find it difficult to get permanent work. Those who live on low incomes are not only unable to afford a home, but have to shift regularly from rented accommodation to rented accommodation according to the whims of landlords and market prices. Even those who have well-paid jobs — indeed, some of those who have top- ranking positions — are involved in a kind of continual migration: within the country, not to it from outside. Many of us are in danger of becoming nomads, modern gypsies, who never put down firm roots in one place.

---

1. On this whole area see further my book, *The Tyranny of Time*, Anzea, 1983 and IVP, 1983

Such people spend much of their time settling in or preparing to move. Even those who stay five or six years in one place hold back from getting too involved in their community, for they know that one day they will be on the move again. Where Christians are concerned, this is often the case with respect to the church.

Older societies which were too static had their own problems. Mobility brings certain advantages. But too much mobility creates other problems and we are now beginning to feel their weight. It breaks up relationships and puts greater pressure upon nuclear family units, pressure under which they frequently crack. It severs people from a sense of place so that they lose touch with their roots and lose sight of the importance of their environment. It cuts them off from certain traditions that would help them negotiate their way more discerningly through life. It curtails their willingness to commit themselves — to other people, to a neighbourhood, to institutions — for it is too costly to take that step and then have to withdraw. Apart from occasional challenges to Christians to be ready to launch out into the unknown for God, we lack any substantial Christian appraisal of mobility.[2]

3. Debt

It may sound strange to talk about the pressure of debt when we live in one of the most affluent countries in the world, especially when we have fewer very rich or very poor people here than in most comparable countries. But we are becoming aware of the increasing public debt our country is accruing and the number of families below the poverty line is also climbing steadily. Such families frequently go into debt because it is the only way they can afford the basic necessities of shelter, food and clothing. Or, at the very least, they find themselves indebted to various charitable organisations and welfare agencies without whom they could not survive.

---

2. One who opens up this subject is J. McInnes, *The New Pilgrims*, Albatross, 1980

But just because many people earn a reasonable amount of money does not mean they are free from debt. On all sides today we are tempted to spend more than we earn. Anyone who has worked in a bank knows how large a proportion of people on very high incomes live from one pay check to the next. Others live off their credit cards and frequently have to arrange for extensions because they have not paid off their purchases in the required time. Many tie up part of their income in advance through buying items that they cannot afford now and paying for them by instalments. In particular, the high cost of housing means that most people are in debt to banks, mortgage societies or finance companies for up to half their lives. The burden this lays upon young people is quite criminal. Few of us realise how much and for how long enslaved we are in this area.

This situation is unfortunate: first, because we do not examine ourselves more to see how much our own greed produces this situation; second, because we put up with social conditions which automatically sentence people to permanent debt who simply want a home to live in; and third, because some people are ashamed to admit how deeply they are involved in debt and therefore do not call for help when they need it. Owning up to their situation would result in too severe a loss of face.

Debt is also unfortunate because it limits people's options, restricting their freedom to do what God wants until they have paid off their mortgage. Their ability to give to others is likewise circumscribed. Debt is one of the main factors making for tension in the family and for breaking up marriages. Squabbles between couples frequently arise over money, or the lack of it. Notions of 'thrift' and 'saving' were part and parcel of the older middle-class Christian tradition, but this is less so today. Warnings against materialism or against the love of money, and encouragements to give generously, still abound in pulpits. But these in themselves do not amount to an adequate Christian approach to money.

4. Other general social pressures in brief

There are other pressures besides the three already mentioned. Some of these are:

(a) Conformity

During the last century that perceptive critic of emerging forms of democracy, Alexis de Toqueville, issued a warning. He foresaw that democracy's rejection of the tyranny of the one or few could still leave it vulnerable to the tyranny of the many. The preferences and patterns of the majority might increasingly squeeze out minority viewpoints. The role of public opinion polls in marketing and politics and the dominance of the mass media, relying as it does so heavily on advertising, are of concern here. Although in some respects we are now beneficiaries of greater pluralism, there are sufficient signs of tendencies to the contrary to trouble us.

(b) Security

The same writer also argued that, when it came to a crisis or a serious choice, people in the newly-emerging democracies would be tempted to place security above freedom. Today, for all our talk of personal independence and regard for civil liberties, we see this happening on an increasing scale. The insurance and banking industry feeds on our desire for security, makes ever more extravagant claims about its capacity to take care of our future and advertises its wares in language as religious as any preacher. In an endangered economy we are also watching the way in which those who have are searching for greater guarantees of security for themselves, even if this means providing less justice for those who have not.

(c) Regulation

We are also observing a growing professionalising and bureaucratising of life. Aspects of life previously looked after by individuals, families or voluntary associations have become the preserve of trained specialists. This has not always been to the advantage of the average person. Areas of life generally ignored by governments have also become subject to more administrative regulation. Again, this has not always been beneficial to the wider public. As a consequence, we are in danger of losing the capacity to take responsibility for and manage many of our own affairs.

The pressures I have mentioned are sufficient to indicate some of the forces which shape us and our society. They also shape our churches and Christian organisations far more than we realise. Just think how busy many churches are, how mobile are their members, and how much they are in debt for buildings they have erected. Unless a theology of everyday life comes to terms with pressures like these, it will only scratch the surface of our lives. Our chief need in the face of such pressures is to begin asking questions about them. Often these pressures go unrecognised, or where they do gain recognition are accepted fatalistically. We need to challenge features of our society which so many people take for granted or regard as inevitable. In this area, asking the hard questions, the questions which very few other people are asking, is the beginning of wisdom.

Routine aspects of life

Much of life is relatively routine. Each day presents us with a round of situations to negotiate and most of the time we do this as a matter of course. If we do not spend as much time worrying about these as we do about the pressures we are under, that does not mean they are unimportant. Now and again these routine matters themselves become problematic. But their significance for us does not rest on this happening. They are significant simply because they are there, an integral part of our lives.

What are some of these routine situations? How fundamental a part do they play in our lives? Do we reflect on them Christianly? Is there a distinctive Christian perspective upon them? Or, if our intentions, motives and goals are right, will they simply fall into place? Before you read what I have to say, take a sheet of paper and write down the fairly regular or routine activities you engage in on a typical weekday and on, say, a Saturday. Go into detail about this: give thought to what you do every quarter hour of the day and evening. This is what people do who are asked to fill out a time-budget survey so that they can know more about where our time goes. Once you have done this, see if you can group your findings under a few general headings that define the broader activities we take part in.

Now let me list, not in any order of importance, a few of the most common routine activities we engage in during the course of a day.

1. Commuting

Most of us spend a reasonable amount of time commuting to and from work. By 'work' I mean not only the activity of those workers who have to travel to and from their jobs, but those going to the shops or to school. It is not generally realised that much of the time gained from shorter working hours or labour-saving devices over the last fifty years has been lost through increased time spent in travelling as cities have expanded. Now that a greater percentage of women are in the workforce, and those women or men who remain home travel further to shop, more people are travelling more of the time than ever before.

Although we rarely think about it, commuting raises a number of important questions. Is it more important to live closer to work, shops and schools in less advantageous surroundings so that the family has more opportunity to be together or is quality of place more important? How much energy do people have especially at the start and end of the day, or how much does their mode of transport allow them, to put commuting time to any profitable use? Where it can be used in this way should it be primarily for socialising, catching up with the news, doing additional work, or given over to reading, reflecting and praying? What can we do about the fact that many of those who can least afford to commute long distances are the ones who often have to do so in order to find work?

Few people have given much thought to the effect of

different kinds of transport on our society as a whole.[3] The advantages of the car are well known and I do not need to labour them here. Nor would I want what follows to be interpreted as a plea for doing away with it. But have you ever considered how far you should patronise public methods of transport, since it is primarily the car which has led to their deterioration and the consequent disadvantaging of the poor, unemployed, incapacitated and aged? While a car may be necessary for some people most of the time and for all of us some of the time, should you limit the number of cars your household runs and have a practical commitment to carpooling? Do you really need a car at all or can you make do with part-ownership of a car with other members of your family or church?

Since the car is the main cause of accidents and deaths in our community, how do we fulfil our responsibility to minimise this carnage? Given that the car is the chief contributor to pollution of the atmosphere, what practical steps can we take to combat this? How effectively do Christians resist the wide-scale idolatry of the car in our society or allow worldly values in this area to mould them into its own image? How justified is it to go into debt to purchase a car and would the money spent on the car — around one quarter of the average person's income — be better employed in other ways? What effect would a drop in the purchase of cars have upon employment in the automobile industry and how far should this influence our decisions in this area?

2. Shopping

If we are to go by the amount of money spent upon advertising, then shopping is perhaps the central activity around which our society revolves. The amount of effort we put into thinking about what to buy is one indicator of this. Shopping is one of our main topics of conversation. Families spend more time on shopping outings than on enjoyment of nature

---

3. But see further I. Illich, *Energy and Equity*, Marion Boyars, 1974

or going to church. By their own admission, newspapers, radio and television primarily exist to advertise goods and services rather than provide news, entertainment and education. Around 75% of newspaper space is given over to advertisements, while commercial radio and television programming is a battle to gain advertisers rather than viewers.

The size and character of the buildings now being constructed for shopping is another sign of its importance. Shopping malls are the new cathedrals of the suburbs, increasingly dominating the geography, road networks, socialising and politics of local communities. Economic considerations dominate these complexes and big companies control much of what goes on inside them. Yet to some extent such malls do provide space for people to gather and for communal activities to take place, just as the media do give us some access to news and information and provide a certain degree of enjoyable entertainment. Buying and selling are also valid activities in themselves and have helped improve not just the quantity but also the quality of life in certain respects.

From one angle, shopping has been accorded substantial Christian attention. For more than a decade, advocates of a simpler lifestyle have challenged people to question their consumer-orientated outlook.[4] Adopting a lower standard of living, they have argued, would help overcome the gap between the poor and the wealthy both within and between countries. It would also result in a better quality of life for those who took this step. But the principle of 'enough is enough' has only gone skin-deep into Christian consciousness and the 'simple lifestyle' analysis does not penetrate sufficiently deeply into the manipulative character, addictive nature and quasi-religious appeal of shopping in our society.

---

4. Among others see the collection of articles ed. R.J. Sider, *Living More Simply: Biblical Principles and Practical Models*, Hodder and Stoughton, 1980

People in marketing and advertising work hard to break down our resistance to the lure of shopping. The architecture, layout, colour scheme and atmosphere of shopping centres are all carefully calculated to entice us to spend. They are also designed to take us out of ourselves, transcend our routine lives and give us a quasi-religious experience. (The newest shopping mall in Darwin is actually patterned upon a basilica, the earliest form of church building.) Through the clothes they buy people are sometimes searching for their own identity or trying to create one they do not have. The quest for bargains and discounts partly arises from a desire to receive something gratuitously, as a matter of 'grace' so to speak. The big purchases people make often stem from their unconscious longing for a 'peak experience' that will bring them a sense of well-being.[5] Quite apart from all this, some people — mainly retired, deserted and disadvantaged people — live under the weekly pressure of not having enough to buy the things that they need. Or are seduced to buy the wrong things or spend beyond what they should apportion to purchased items.

3. Sleeping
At the beginning of this book I mentioned the importance of developing a theology of sleep. We need to do this partly because so much of our lives is taken up with sleep. But sleep is important in itself. It is not just a withdrawal from activity. Important physical, psychological and spiritual processes are at work while we are lying in bed. Alongside the physical rest our bodies benefit from in sleep, we all dream and all dream much more than we suppose. Unless we did so we would be unable to cope with waking life. Dreams enable us to absorb and come to terms with many of the events we have encountered during the day. Some of these dreams

---

5. See especially the essays on 'Shopping World : The Palace of Modern Consumption' and 'The Fur Hat' in J. Carroll, *Sceptical Sociology*, Routledge and Kegan Paul, 1980

reveal aspects of ourselves which our conscious mind will not admit. God also reveals to us through dreams — or sometimes by means of a vision or voice — things he wishes us to know and to do. The Bible is full of such incidents. So are the lives of people in non-Western societies. It is only those in Western society who discount the importance of these phenomena or who have lost the capacity to interpret them.

Other thoughts are prone to come to our minds before we go to sleep at night or before we get up in the morning. Sometimes in these rare moments of quiet we are put in touch with our deepest longings and receive hints about our basic vocation. Or we lie awake planning and plotting to our own advantage, sometimes even masking this with a veneer of spirituality, rather than entrusting ourselves in sleep to God. Many people, and you may be one of them, find it difficult to sleep properly today. This may stem from the amount of work you choose to do and the hectic pace at which you live. It may stem from the amount of work you are forced to do and the number of responsibilities you have to carry. Insomnia is now the most widespread disability in Western countries and is seriously affecting people's physical, emotional, mental and spiritual capacities. We need to identify not only its personal and social causes, as certain writers are already doing, but its spiritual roots as well. The Bible has something to say about this, in passages which are often overlooked or deliberately ignored.

4. Other routine aspects of life in brief
I have considered only three routine aspects of life that require serious Christian consideration. There are many others that I could mention. Let me briefly mention a number of more specific activities:

(a) Eating and drinking
The nature, enjoyment and purpose of cooking; the role of meals in family life; the importance of hospitality; the religious dimension of the ordinary meal; the vulgarisation of eating and drinking in modern society; the meal as an expres-

sion of our concern for, and inclusion of, the lonely and needy; the role of traditional extended family meals, such as birthdays and Christmas; the rejuvenation of wider and narrower family celebrations.

(b) Dress

The problem of fashion — dress as a status symbol in modern society; the problem of mass conformity — and mass non-conformity — in dress; the exploitation of workers in the clothing industry; the significance of home-made as well as shop-bought clothes; the extent to which clothes should be an expression of the individual; the extent to which clothes should be an indicator of public function; the use of clothes for sexual differentiation or titillation; the inordinate amounts of money spent on clothing; the validity or invalidity of regimentation of clothing in some institutions; the need to do away with distinctions of dress in the church.

(c) Hospitality

Importance of people having a space of their own into which they can invite others; the gift of hospitality as one of the manifestations of the Spirit and ways in which it can be developed; the reasons for the contraction of hospitality in our society; the problem of homelessness among the young, refugees and physically abused; the ministry of hospitality to the lonely, the disadvantaged and the ostracised; the role of hospitality in evangelism in the early church and today; the ministry of hospitality to the lonely, the disadvantaged and the ostracised; the home as the basic location for gathering as church; home designing and decoration as a context for people's art; the role of communal living or of including in your home one who has no close family relationships.

(d) Hobbies

The rise of the hobby as a compensation for the monotony of work; the hobby as a more meaningful form of work; the relationship between the hobby and leisure; the mass production of hobbies and the demise of the self-created activity; the hobby as an escape from family and social responsibilities; the hobby as the development of a creative gift and how to stimulate it in those whom society views as failures.

(e) Gardening

The link between God's creation of and care for the world and gardening; gardening as a means of retaining a link with nature in an urban environment; gardening as fulfilling a responsibility to future generations; the temptation to turn gardening into an all-absorbing preoccupation; the garden as a context for parables from God; the possibilities in gardening for sharing with the poor; gardening as a self-help task for the retired and unemployed; the importance of public gardens in an urban or suburban landscape; the implications of the importance of gardens for housing policy and housing developments.

On work and leisure
1. Work
Once again I am using the word 'work' in a wider sense than is usually understood. Work embraces:

* paid employment
* housework
* schoolwork and study
* voluntary work

and we need a theology of all these. Here again you might like to think first what you would list here if you were writing this section. Go over in your mind your own work situation, whatever that might be, and try to define the main issues that it raises for you. Some of these might arise out of your own choice or circumstances; others might be forced upon you by those whom you work for or be felt as outside impositions even by them. When you have done this, see how similar or different your lists are.

It is now clear that the more people spend their time in a certain environment the more they will be shaped by that environment. In our kind of society, the work environment is, for some, the most total and life-encompassing institution, often more so than the family. It is where many find their identity, status and power. It significantly affects their views and values. The influence of the work environment explains why people who have similar occupations so often think, talk, behave and even dress alike. Since work is the main reality for many of us, we test much else that we experience by judgments we form through it. As yet, we have scarcely begun to come to terms with the all-pervasive effect that the work environment has on the way most of us look at life and conduct ourselves. As we have seen, it can even modify or undermine religious beliefs and values.

Here are some of the questions we need to address:

☐ How can work, wherever it takes place, become a less secularising experience? What can be done to help Christians compartmentalise their lives less between church and work or between their inner and outer selves at work?

☐ What should motivate our choice of a particular occupation? Should it be motivated by a sense of meaningfulness, fulfilment, service, ministry? How far should we be influenced by educational results, others' pressure, financial reward or status considerations?

☐ Where do those who wish to conduct their work in a more responsible way find the resources and support to do this?

☐ How possible is it to develop a set of standards for occupations, professions, companies, industries or departments that will meet with common consent?

☐ What should employers and what can employees do about the unreal pressures and expectations which exist in so much paid employment?

☐ How far is excellence and promotion an achievable and desirable goal and to what extent are the two compatible?

☐ What are the limits to our obedience and accountability to our employers and what are their responsibilities to their employees?

☐ How do we deal with the problem of abusive and discriminatory language at work, double standards, favouritism and obstructionism, or peer pressure to do less work than is approriate?

☐ What is the responsibility of Christians who belong to a union in terms of seeking office in it, responding to calls for passive or militant action and making their opinions felt when unions appear to go too far or not far enough?

☐ What responsibility do Christian employers and employees have to discover creative, perhaps even unpopular, ways of generating new jobs and alleviating the unemployment problem?

☐ How can we encourage people to see their work in the context of God's providential ordering of life in the world and discover the implications of this for organisations, households and individuals?

☐ Are the churches themselves at the forefront of pioneering new approaches to work that will lead people into new patterns and types of worthwhile activity, even if these are voluntary in nature and outside the structures of paid employment?

☐ How can we give people a sense of the value of their work irrespective of the amount they are paid for it?

☐ Can housework be integrated into a genuinely Christian vision of life that does not idolise or belittle it, entertain myths about technology's time-saving contribution, or restrict it to the woman's sphere?[6]

☐ How harmful or beneficial is it, by means of the emphasis upon homework, to inculcate into children the idea of bringing work home at the end of the day?

Once again I am not trying to be exhaustive. There are other questions that could be asked about the size of many work environments, such as bureaucracies. How much power should be given to those bureaucracies, such as multinational corporations, which are based abroad or to associations of people involved in work, such as trade unions? From

---

6. Helpful starting points here are provided by K.A. Rabuzzi, *Toward a Theology of Housework*, 1982

your own experience of work I am sure that you could add other questions to this list.

Happily, some of these issues are now being addressed by Christian thinkers and writers, as well as by small groups of Christians in their workplaces. This is beginning to provide a broader definition of what we should regard as work and a clearer understanding of how we should view and do our work.[7] We are also beginning to see a more concerted effort to analyse and combat a related problem, large-scale unemployment. In some measure this is now here to stay and there is no simple solution to it. It will be a fact of life well into the future and we have to prepare ourselves and our children for it, as well as find ways of minimising it where we can. There is a need for experiment in this area, as well as reflection if we are to make any substantial inroads into the problem.

2. Leisure

Below is a list of some high priority leisure pursuits:
* walking, climbing, hiking
* playing, games, sports
* swimming, surfing, sailing
* driving, riding, boating
* picnicking, camping, caravaning
* travel and tourism

For only one of these do I know of a carefully and joyously developed theological appraisal.[8]

For most people leisure is a central part of their lives. As Ronald Conway points out in the title of his book *The Land of the Long Weekend*, leisure is most important to Australians. This is also true for New Zealanders. We have more public holidays, a greater number of long weekends and longer vacations than people in any comparable society. A large

---

7. On some of these issues see, inter alia, P. Marshall, E. Vanderkloet, P. Nijkamp, S. Griffioen and H. Antonides in *Labour of love: Essays on work*, Wedge, 1980

8. T. Slater, *The Temporary Community*, Albatross, 1984 on camping.

proportion of West Coast Canadians and Americans likewise prefer increased leisure time to higher income. While in parts of the US many people live in order to work, here many more work in order to live. For some years now, forecasters have predicted the arrival of the 'leisure society'. Urban planners and companies have conducted many surveys to find out what we might want to do with the extra time at our disposal. We can also take courses to prepare us to use our leisure constructively. For some time governments have been appointing ministers of sport and recreation to develop these more fully. Local councils increasingly seek to provide for the leisure needs of the young people in their district.

Yet most people have less leisure than they are told or imagine. The rhythms of work carry over into their leisure time so that they cannot really enjoy it as they would like. I have also noted that economic circumstances or social disadvantages sometimes prevent people from experiencing the leisure they need. There is an ongoing tendency to turn leisure activities into things at which people work hard or through which they feel pressured. We have also watched the growth of giant leisure industries to cater for our wants in this area. Leisure has become a multi-million dollar industry which carefully manipulates the way in which we spend our free time. There are many issues that require attention here. I invite you to enumerate those which occur to you.

Beyond the issues I have already raised in connection with sport, I list the following:

☐ From a Christian point of view, do we work primarily to have leisure or have leisure primarily to refresh ourselves for work?

☐ What is leisure anyway, and how far does it overlap with or differ from what we describe as 'free-time'?

☐ How much real 'rest' do people get during their time off from work?

☐ Is 'play' equivalent to 'sport' and, if not, what kind of balance should be struck between the two?

- ☐ Have many sporting activities become more competitive and how much is this a good thing?
- ☐ How much should we encourage children to engage in non-competitive games and play as opposed to competitive sport?
- ☐ How self-initiating or technologically dependent, and how spontaneous or programmed, should leisure activities be?
- ☐ What balance should be struck between appreciating the creation around us and developing the creative gifts we have been given?
- ☐ Do weekend church activities help or hinder the 'rest' the Bible encourages us to enjoy?
- ☐ Where do meditation and contemplation fit in to time spent in leisure?
- ☐ How much should leisure be a corporate and not merely individual or family affair? How much should church members play together?
- ☐ How can the sabbath principle or inner rest which God enjoys be more fully experienced by and made available to Christians?

These are by no means the only questions that need to be pursued. For example, how much should governments be permitted to spend on producing elite athletes rather than making provisions for all people to engage in some sport? How can pressure be brought to bear so that control of the media is decentralised and greater access given to a range of community and other groups? Does there need to be a revision of many sporting codes to encourage more responsible attitudes to the games they regulate? Other issues include the way in which holidays can be most fruitfully taken and the role of the sabbatical year or long-service leave in discovering where one is heading in life. There is also the major question of retirement in a society in which people are increasingly living longer. This is a vast area in itself and one that needs more and more of our attention. The provision of church homes and services for the aged is a real contribution here. But it is only the outer edge of a large tract of unexplored territory.[9]

Central features of modern life

I would like now to discuss several important aspects of modern life which we do well to understand and confront. Since these are more diffuse in character than the matters I have mentioned to this point, it would be more difficult to ask you to test your own perceptions against mine. Again I will only refer to a number of areas and briefly indicate why I think each is important.

1. Popular attitudes and values

We have many statistical studies of the attitudes and values of ordinary Australians. These are helpful to a point, but they do not go very deep. Only in-depth interviews begin to reveal the full character of people's outlooks, the actual strength of their convictions and the complex, paradoxical and even contradictory nature of many of their views. Public opinion polls, census figures and studies such as the Australian Values Survey can only take us so far. They give us a surface reading of what we as a people are thinking, choosing and doing. That is why more substantial investigations, such as the Practices and Beliefs Survey now under way in Australia, are important. But we need more than this. There are quite simple yet profound questions we can all ask. What are the things that make the average person in our society:
 laugh and cry?
 hope and despair?
 believe and doubt?
 share and withdraw?
 love and hate?
 trust and fear?
The only place to begin here is with ourselves and with those

---

9. R.K. Johnston, *The Christian at Play*, Eerdmans, 1983, discusses certain approaches to leisure in a helpful way.

closest to us. I know of no better way to begin to know our-selves and others more closely and we will find out things by this means that no survey or commentator can discover.[10]

Even when we have a fuller picture of what is going on inside the minds, hearts and imaginations of ordinary Aus-tralians, the hardest work is still to be done. We need to know how to bring the light of the gospel to bear upon their:

images of reality,

the motives they display,

the values they live by,

the beliefs they entertain,

the goals they have.

These are the difficult questions to answer. Attempts to interpret the meaning of some of the data assembled in the comparative sociological studies of attitudes and preferences in different countries by Hans Mol and others are very helpful.[11] But we still know too little. And such interpreta-tions tend to be either too individual or purely sociological in character. In both areas we have taken only a few steps down what is a rather long road.

2. Communicating and relating

Communication takes place in a number of different ways in our society. Apart from the not unimportant non-verbal forms of communication, there is:

conversation,

discussion,

instruction,

---

10. For America one could start with R. Bellah et al., *Habits of the Heart* and for Australia, J. Fiske et al., *The Myths of Oz*

11. See H. Mol, et al., *Western Religion*, Morton, 1972, and on Australia, *The Faith of Australians*, Allen and Unwin, 1985; Practice and Belief, *A. Black and P. Glasner (eds), Allen and Unwin, 1983* as well as D. Millikan, The Sunburnt Soul: Christianity in Search of an Australian Identity, *Anzea, 1981 and B. Wilson,* Can God Survive in Australia?, *Albatross, 1983*

letter-writing,
telephoning,
reading,
mass media.

With the exception of the third and the last, we do not have any developed Christian understanding of these.

Relating and communicating also go on in different contexts, defined by the places or spaces we inhabit. These also require consideration, especially settings in which genuine relationships are forged and real communication goes on. I am thinking here of:

the house or apartment,
the street or neighbourhood,
the mall or restaurant,
the workplace or club,
the park or centre,
the campsite or holiday house,

as well as more intermittent meetings, such as while travelling.

There are a number of issues connected with communication that we need to address. Given the prevalence of superficial media presentations and unexamined peer group opinions, how far are we succumbing to propaganda and prejudices rather than forming properly thought-out views? What about the fact that less powerful groups in society — ethnic groups, native peoples, the aged — do not get as much representation as others? How high on our agenda, even in Christian families and churches, is the creation of space for informed and critical conversation on matters of importance? How much time or energy do we have at the end of a day or over a weekend to read the material that would help us form sound judgments about a whole range of matters? These are only some of the questions we should be asking and answering. For we are in real danger in our universally educated society of producing people who are uninformed about many of the major issues that affect our lives.

As we are all aware, relationships are under stress in our

society. Marriages are breaking up at an ever-increasing rate, parents and children are seeing less and less of one another as each group pursues its own self-fulfilment, individuals in peer groups are becoming more narcissistic and friends find it hard to clear time to enjoy each other's company in regular and leisurely ways. Symptoms of this deterioration are not difficult to identify. One example is the decline in letter-writing, especially of long, reflective letters to people at a great distance, something which long distance telephone calls can only partly replace.

There has also been a demise in extended day-, weekend- or vacation-long visits between friends. In fact we need to revivify the whole notion of friendship for it is in serious danger of becoming superficial. The problem of lack of communication within marriage or among families is happily better served from a Christian point of view, though even much of what is said fails to come to grips with the realities of married life and with the effects of changes in working, social and urban patterns upon couples and children today.

3. Social rituals and activities

There are a number of rituals in our society about which there has been very little Christian reflection. Think, for example, of the following:

(a) Enforced waiting

One of the ironies of our society, which is obsessed with speed, is the amount of time we spend waiting, queuing or sitting in traffic jams. Waiting is one of our least acknowledged rituals. If we do spend up to five percent of our lives waiting for one reason or another, surely we ought to have some understanding of why this happens, what we can do about it and how or whether we should spend the time more fruitfully.

(b) Family events

We still tend to celebrate family events such as birthdays, engagements and anniversaries in conventional ways without giving much thought to how they could be enhanced

Christianly. Other events such as the birth of children, obtaining a job, moving to another city, purchase of a house, coming-of-age and retirement are rarely celebrated in a way that does them justice from a Christian point of view.

(c) Popular rites

Weekly rituals, like the late shopping night or Saturday morning outing to the mall, are often a family affair. What is or is not going on when this is taking place and how much does it enhance our lives or replace more significant family rituals? The barbecue is another well-known Australian ritual, perhaps declining in popularity but still significant. There are also those habitually and culturally legitimate opportunities for gambling — connected with betting, poker machines and lotteries — that so attract sections of the population. Do we know why this rite is so popular and how much it symbolises the main forces and preoccupations in our society? Do we know what will most attract others to put their risk-taking instincts to more constructive use?

(d) Club membership

Clubs are very prolific in modern society. In my own city there are over three hundred different types, ranging from the large clubs based on sport, nationality or returned servicemen to the small associations centred on some hobby or interest. Yet clubs also existed in large numbers in the first century. The early Christians had to come to terms with them, as passages in the New Testament bear witness. How do we understand, evaluate and respond to the phenomenon of the club? In what ways do clubs make a social contribution or harmfully influence their members? What possibilities do they offer for communicating the gospel or gathering as church? We might also consider how far congregations have themselves become simply religious clubs.

(e) Civic celebrations

Apart from church services associated with particular ceremonies, and occasional participation by Christians in city festivals, how much have we thought about involving ourselves in such happenings? We are part of a larger community and from time to time should celebrate what we have in common. Should we perhaps seek ways of enhancing civic occasions? So many of them turn most people into spectators and we could help make them more participatory. How can we as congregations celebrate and — in view of our treatment of Aborigines — lament the founding of our nation? We have hardly any traditions to follow here.

4. Secular idols and religions

In the West we have a particular fascination with objects. In fact, we tend to value things more than people. Some of the objects are central to the operation of our society and therefore become symbols of what we most highly prize. These objects receive an enormous amount of attention. They are the locus of a whole range of expectations. Yet they are also a source of frustration and have many disruptive and harmful effects. In other words they have all the characteristics of *idols*. If the following items were not so difficult to avoid noting as you read this, I would suggest that you make your own list and compare it with mine. I doubt whether there would be many differences. These are the ones that came to my mind, most of them fairly readily:

the watch
the diary
the credit card
the telephone
the computer
the television set
the car
the home.

For all their centrality in modern life, all these but the last have received surprisingly little attention from Christian thinkers. I have written at length about some of these — the watch, diary and telephone — elsewhere.[12] I have also said something about others — the credit card and car — earlier

---

12. See again *The Tyranny of Time*, Anzea, 1983 and IVP, 1983

in this book. The television set and the computer have received, or are beginning to receive, thoughtful Christian attention.[13] While I have mentioned the home briefly already, in connection with debt, I would like to add a little here.

The home occupies a special place in our lives. It is part of the Australian dream and more of us are able to fulfil the dream of home ownership than is possible anywhere else in the world. But the dream has a way of becoming a nightmare. Many people can no longer afford a home and even rented accommodation is becoming less available or less permanent. Others are being turned out of their homes and have nowhere to live. We are seduced into thinking that a satisfying life is impossible unless we own a home that accords with the latest expectations and sacrifice more of our money, time and energy to it than we give to other people or needs. We turn it into a monastic retreat from the world rather than a creative bridgehead into it. We think individualistically about it and do not consider ways in which we can cooperate in designing, financing, building and living in homes that have a more modest and more communal character. Our decisions in this area often result in unnecessary delay in having children, in unfortunate clustering in more advantaged parts of the city and in unhelpfully increasing already congested traffic.

In varying degrees, all the objects I have mentioned, allowing for the many benefits they have bestowed upon us, threaten to shape us more than we control them. They are significant pointers to the main substitute religions. Although these substitute religions are fairly well known, too often we merely denounce them, failing to see that we are often caught up in them ourselves. Those religions are:

    material possessions
    guaranteed security

13. For example by D. Lyon, *The Silicon Society*, Hodder and Stoughton, 1986

    the family
    educational achievement
    work and sport
    fitness and health
    self and sexual fulfilment.

The extent to which Christians are vulnerable to these substitute religions is a matter for careful reflection. Even though they might attempt to resist crasser pressures to become consumer-orientated, Christians are easily tempted to join the treasure hunt for the best discounts, sales and clearances and turn these into a central feature of their thinking and conversation. They are in danger of treating the nuclear family as an idol, neglecting the biblical role of the extended natural family or extended Christian family, of the church within the church. Christians are as vulnerable as anyone to loading expectations upon their children about educational advancement through the 'best' schools, despite the pressure it brings upon the need for both parents to work and the effect this often has on the quality of family life.

Though Christians may have repudiated any approach to God based on justification by works, they can easily be caught up in an attempt to prove their worth and acceptability to others and themselves, even partially to God, through their work. Keeping healthy and fit is entirely proper, especially in chair-bound and car-imprisoned society, but there is always a danger of giving more time and attention to this than to relationships, with God as much as others. So pervasive is the belief that happiness is one of the goals we should have in life, that it is almost impossible for us to escape altogether the feverish search for self-fulfilment, especially if it is cloaked in the language of charismatic experiences or spiritual exercises. So then, while all these aspects of life are legitimate in themselves, we must exercise care lest they become ends in themselves rather than means, and not necessarily means for all of us, towards other more fundamental ends.

Conclusion

I would like to give the concluding word to Jaques Ellul who, more than anyone writing at present, has made the most trenchant plea for every aspect of our lives to be drawn into a Christian pattern of understanding:

It is evident that the first thing to do is to be faithful to revelation, but this fidelity can only become a reality in daily life through the creation of a new way of life: this is the 'missing link'. There used to be a style of life peculiar to the Middle Ages. In the sixteenth century there was a style of life carried on by Reformed Church Christians, and it is extremely interesting to note where it differed from the style of life of the Renaissance. There is the bourgeois style of life, which has no spiritual quality at all; there is the Communist style of life; there is no longer a Christian style of life. To speak quite frankly, without beating about the bush, a doctrine only has power (apart from that which God gives it) to the extent to which it creates a style of life, to the extent to which it is adopted, believed and accepted by people who have a style of life which is in harmony with it...

... if we consider the life of Christians in our churches, we see certainly that they make good sons, fathers, husbands, employers and workmen. They have many individual virtues but they have no style of life, or rather, they have exactly that which has been imposed upon them by their sociological conditions: that is to say, by their social class, their nation, their environment and so on. It is not their spiritual condition which affects their style of life: it is their political or economic condition, and from this point of view, they are an overwhelming demonstration of the truth, temporary and temporal, of Marxism. Now at the present time, many Christians are fully aware that this is an intolerable situation, and that if it is allowed to go on, it will prepare the way for the total collapse of the churches in the West. The problem of the style of life is absolutely central: for it is at this point that the question of the integration of Christianity into the world, or at least of its creative power, will be most fiercely tested...

The creation of such a style of life is a work which is both collective and individual. It is a fact for each Christian who really tries to express his faith in the concrete forms of his life. It is also the task of Christians as a corporate body, where all these efforts, sometimes differing widely, sometimes even contradictory, are recorded... as its name indicates, the whole of life is concerned in this search. It includes the way we think about present political questions, as well as our way of practising hospitality. It also affects the way we dress and the food we eat (...the problems of taste, fashion, cooking, are important if we are to form a style of life...) as well as the way in which we manage our financial affairs. It includes being faithful to one's wife as well as being accessible to one's neighbour. It includes the position one ought to take on current social questions, as well as the decisions which relate to the personal employment of our time.

I could multiply these examples, which are mere suggestions, to show that absolutely everything, the smallest details which we regard as indifferent, ought to be questioned, placed in the light of faith, examined from the point of view of the glory of God.[14]

In this chapter I have identified some of the everyday situations which we need to approach with greater understanding. As I have stressed throughout, these are not the only aspects of everyday life that require consideration. In particular I have said little about some of the life stages people pass through — from birth, through marriage to death — and some of the moral dilemmas that people face from time to time — divorce, abortion, homosexuality — many of which are discussed in works of pastoral or applied theology. As generally in the past, these areas of concern do form part of the wider Christian consciousness and in recent times, in Australia as well as elsewhere, there have been some excellent treatments of them. It is because these areas are so much part and parcel of private life that they have been less

---

14. J. Ellul, *The Presence of the Kingdom*, SCM, 1951, pp.145-148

ignored than many other matters. I have also said little about some of the social issues which are important today — racial discrimination and poverty — and some of the political threats which overhang us — government centralisation and nuclear extinction. But that is because these are already receiving some attention by Christian thinkers. The renewed interest in Christians' social responsibilities has ensured this and they must continue to receive the most serious consideration. But much of the time there is less we can do about these directly than many of the matters I have mentioned.

4

The reality principle

I HAVE IDENTIFIED certain aspects of everyday life that we could attend to more closely. How is it possible for any individual, you might ask, to deal with all these issues? Where do I find the time? What should have priority for me? How do I cope in the meantime with not being able to work through other matters? It will help if you bear two things in mind.

First, we do not have to tackle these issues on our own. In fact, it is impossible for us to do so. Only if we tackle them with others will we find the wisdom and strength to do so. Alone they will prove too much: together they are manageable, not only because we will get further if we work together, but because different ones among us will work at different issues so that each one does not have to grapple with all. To do this, however, we have to overcome that individualism which infects our society. It is because we expect to have to do everything ourselves that we are sometimes overwhelmed by all that there is to do.

Second, we do not have to find answers straightaway. We tend to want quick answers to our questions, but quick answers are often superficial. It takes time to discern the truth and we should not feel under pressure about this, certainly not from God. He has structured us so that in all aspects of our life — physically, emotionally, intellectually and spiritually — we take time to reach maturity. So we should take the long-term view and be content with the small but regular progress we are able to make. In any case we will intuitively find answers to some of our questions in the area of everyday life long before we can put these into words. Sometimes our thinking is behind our acting and we know more than we can tell.

But we do need criteria in order to select which issues we should concentrate on. What are these criteria? I think there are two basic ones. First, if as Christians we are seeking to serve our families, friends, fellow Christians and others, what is most relevant to them? Second, what is most relevant to us, at this moment? These two questions will not only provide us with a starting point, but will provide new issues as we go along.

The next question to be tackled is: Where can we best do this? This opens up a number of related issues. Which contexts for learning are the most suitable? How much or how little structure do we require? To what extent can existing patterns of Christian and theological education provide what is needed? Who will develop new models and what should they look like?

There are also a number of practical issues. Should we take time to reflect on everyday matters while continuing our regular commitments or should we also take extended time out from these so we can give them more concentrated attention? Who can provide us with the basic resources that we need — those with formal theological qualifications or those with practical wisdom in the area under discussion? What group processes are best designed to take us where we wish to go? How much do we require a supportive as well as a thoughtful group to enable us to do this?

These are not the only issues to consider, but they are some of the most important. Unless we take them seriously, existing methods and attitudes will prevail by default. This would be a pity, if only because such methods and attitudes are not adequate to attain their own stated goals. In what follows I shall suggest a variety of ways in which we can develop more appropriate structures and attitudes that are more conducive to developing a Christian approach to every-day life. All of them have been worked out and put into prac-tice. Some have sprung out of my own work and I have seen others at first-hand or been involved in them.

The value of churching at home

Involvement in a home church — whether within a congrega-tion or not — can make a significant contribution to develop-ing a Christian understanding of everyday life. I have already mentioned that my interest in home churches partly devel-oped out of the search for a form for the church which brought it closer to everyday life. For me there is a direct connection between the two. As we shall see in a moment, others have come to the same conclusion through starting from the problems of everyday life and searching for a cor-porate way of resolving them.

Since the word is used so loosely today, I need to define what I mean when I say *home church.* I have in mind small, informal extended Christian family units which meet for church in a home. Sometimes these are independent of any denomination, sometimes they belong to one. Whatever the case, those who gather in homes for church also gather regu-larly in a larger meeting, either with a cluster of independent home churches every so often or every week with other members of their congregation.[1] What does involvement in a home church have to do with thinking Christianly about everyday life? And why have I begun with reference to this? The best way to explain this is to draw on the experience of William Diehl who became increasingly aware of the gap between his religious and workaday worlds while he was a senior executive in a major US steel corporation. He also regretted the fact that his church had not helped him to bridge this gap. Towards the end of his book, *Christianity and Real Life,* Diehl describes how he began to find an answer:

1. For further information see Robert and Julia Banks, *The Church Comes Home: A New Base for Community and Mission,* Albatross, 1989, expecially chapter 10.

In recent years a form of local grouping has emerged. We call it the 'house church' and it is almost universally a lay-initiated phenomenon ... The name of our house church is *Focus*... it consists of twenty-three adults and twenty children. Six of the families are active members in traditional church parishes representing three denominations. Seven of the families formerly were active in the church, but dropped out due to the failure of their congregations to provide the kind of support they felt was necessary in relating faith to life today... There are two former clergymen in the group, but their role is the same as that of any other member in the group. In areas of biblical knowledge they do have more expertise, but then our scientist members have greater skills in their respective fields also. Those families which are still associated with the institutional church all agree that *Focus* has provided their lives with a dimension of Christian community which they have been unable to find in their traditional congregations.

The general operational style of *Focus* has changed very little during the past five years. Every other Sunday morning the total community gathers at the faculty house of a local college for breakfast and a worship-study period. Families take turns providing the simple breakfast and leading the morning program... Worship in the *Focus* community is relevant to the real-life experiences of the group and springs from the innermost thoughts and concerns of all its members. The educational period, which is woven into or follows the worship experience, is also designed by the same parents and children. Generally, a theme has been established by the community to extend over several sessions. For example, over a period of several months we studied various families in the Bible, with each of us selecting a favourite Bible family and presenting a learning session on it. Frequently, the educational periods involve such things as role-playing, small group discussion, skits, and use of visual aids. Efforts are made for the study periods to have an experiential dimension to them... While these learning periods may lack the comprehensive content of institutionally designed curriculum material, they far exceed parish religious education experiences in freshness, excitement and total involvement of people... I believe the example we set before our children as we struggle to learn about our faith and share it with the rest of the community is a far more enduring type of learning than that which most children get in their parish Sunday schools.

On alternate Sunday evenings, the adult members of *Focus* gather in a home for discussion, study, sharing of life experiences and providing of mutual support. At times the group may review a religious book or essay. Sometimes there will be a series of evenings devoted to study of topics of current interest... The style of our evenings together is such that the agenda can readily be switched to that which is needed by one of the members. A member of the community is thus free to bring up anything that is happening in his or her life which he or she would like to share with friends... Not only are individuals able to share their concerns with the rest of the group, they can rely on support from the other members... Thus the sharing of family problems, of job concerns, of town and neighbourhood service efforts, or of other personal experiences provides effective support and love for the individual members unlike anything I have ever experienced in a traditional congregation.[2]

Diehl concludes by emphasising that the house church phenomenon is a grassroots response to the credibility gap between belief and daily life that many Christians experience. It is a 'bottom-up' rather than 'top-down' affair, one discovered and designed for the most part by ordinary Christians themselves. He points out that it is also an informal rather than formal approach to the problem, which allows people's own experiences to dictate the agenda and for learning to take place through group discussion and study. He stresses the importance of the 'supportive' as well as more specifically 'educational' character of the group, for translating faith into action also requires others' encouragement and prayer. Such a group also has a unique contribution

---

2. W. Diehl, op.cit., p.97ff

to make to character formation, which is vital since the mere acquisition of knowledge is not sufficient of itself to alter behaviour patterns. For these and other reasons, I am convinced that some kind of home church experience is fundamental to developing an integrated Christian approach to life.

Other study groups or action groups can produce some of the same benefits, but they are less holistic in their effects and do not tend to create the same climate of trust and promote the same level of sharing of day-to-day situations. Where you cannot belong to a home church, such groups are a partial compensation. Occasionally membership in two groups, one a close support group and one a practical study group, can provide a measure of the same experience. Where you wish to belong to a home church but do not know of one you can join, you might think of starting one, either in your own congregation or among people who attend different local churches. In itself belonging to a home church is not enough. As I shall go on to explain, we need to place ourselves in other learning contexts as well if we wish to bring our faith to bear upon all the business of life in an effective way. Where it is possible to do so, however, linking up with a home church is the best starting point.

One role-model is worth a hundred instructions

We learn the most fundamental things in life by having them modelled to us by significant others. Often we are not aware how much we do learn this way. We are not always conscious how much we are beginning to imitate others' behaviour. The basic unit of our society, the family, is built upon this kind of learning. In a good family situation children pick up many of the beliefs and values of their parents, even their mannerisms and tone of voice. Modelled learning also takes place in more specialised contexts. Think, for example, of the prophetic bands in the Old Testament, of Jesus' relationship with the Twelve and of the group around Paul involved in his work. Unfortunately, modelled learning has been displaced in most Christian circles by the schooling or academic approach. Although the prophetic, discipling and apostolic model was chiefly designed for people in long-term common work, it has and can still operate with people who come together more intermittently.

In certain respects this approach to learning is similar to that which goes under the name of 'apprenticeship' or 'discipleship' in some charismatic or conservative Christian circles. But both of these contain features which are either opposed to or absent from what I have in mind. For example, they tend to have an anti-intellectual and authoritarian element. For them, while learning the Bible is important, developing a more systematic understanding of how Christianity relates to life is not. While techniques of spiritual development, personal evangelism and church growth are given attention, understanding of the wider social and cultural context is generally overlooked. While there is a close relationship between teacher and pupil, there is a tendency for leaders to reproduce others in their own likeness rather than enable them to find their own ministry. In any case the 'apprenticeship' model is rarely employed with Christians who are not proceeding to more church-related forms of ministry and the 'discipleship' model concentrates more on the inner life and on evangelism than on a wider range of concerns.

Unfortunately, outside the family, where it is becoming increasingly narrowed anyway, there are few areas in secular life where modelling plays a significant part in the learning process. Until fairly recent times it was present in a number of occupations, such as nursing, but now these are also placing more emphasis upon formal rather than on-the-job training. In areas of life where overtones of the master/apprentice relationship remain, as in post-graduate supervision or in manual training, the relationship between the two tends to be rather circumscribed, even where both are Christians.

How then might modelled learning take place in connec-

tion with everyday life issues? Not so long ago I took a
number of people from the church cluster to which I belong
on a ten-day visit to another city. This arose from an invitation to my wife and myself to help an inner-city congregation
think through the pressures of time in everyday life, as well
as related matters concerning lifestyle, relationships and
spirituality. Up to a few years ago I normally accepted such
invitations and handled them alone. But now I always ask if
I can bring a team with me. As a group we plan and prepare
for such visits. We run them together, presenting our material in a variety of ways and in a variety of combinations.
After we return home, we evaluate what we have done and
talk about what we have gained from it. Frequently members
of the team learn new things themselves and develop a
greater coherence in their beliefs. They also discover new
ways of communicating their beliefs and experience a
greater confidence in sharing them.

Several days after our return from an earlier trip — involving ten days with a congregation and two days with a clergy
group, focussing on ways of creating community in the local
church — I was sufficiently struck by the effect of these
visits upon those who came with us to write the following:

> Earlier in the year Julie and I had wanted to run a course so
> that a number of people involved in our groups could deepen
> their understanding of the nature and role of the church. But
> we have not yet had the opportunity to do this and we were
> not sure how to do it in a way that would be fresh and practi-
> cal. We now realise that those who came with us to take part
> in the time with the congregation and clergy group had a the-
> ological learning experience of the most vital and profound
> kind. In both places, though at different levels, Julie and I
> were able to go through a wide range of material, presenting
> it in fresh ways and relating it to the situations of our hearers.
> The other members of the team were able to contribute in
> both settings out of their knowledge and experience and
> found that doing so clarified many things for them. They also
> found that observing and hearing us in action, at times in

ways new to them, enabled both their understanding of the church and ability to talk about it to be enhanced. They have come home very excited about this. The experience has also enabled them to feel the power of what they believe and see its relevance to other churches. This suggests to us that, rather than thinking of running a course on the subject, we should seek to involve more people in such exercises so that they too can learn in the same holistic way.

Various aspects of everyday life could be handled in the same way. But this is also open for others, whose main ministry is through their paid employment or work at home. For example, if you have built up considerable experience of your occupation or profession as well as a Christian perspective upon it, you could give time to helping younger Christians in the same line of work to develop a Christian framework for and approach to their job. This could be done relatively informally through inviting people into your own home or, where possible, through lunch-hour discussions at or near to your work. There you could open up about some of the dilemmas, mistakes and insights you have experienced and talk about common problems. More importantly you could build up a relationship with these people and exemplify the qualities they need to imitate. One of the contributing factors to the uncertainty that many younger Christians face in public life today is lack of adequate role models.[3]

Becoming a member of a task force

Several years ago I became involved with a small group of senior federal public servants who wished to develop a Christian perspective upon their work. We came together through the agency of a centre committed to helping people in the workforce relate their faith to their occupation. We met for a series of preliminary sessions, over breakfast or lunch, to

---

3. There is a brief discussion of the importance of modelling learning in L.O. Richards, *A Theology of Christian Education*, Zondervan, 1975, pp.30-50, 80-87

work out how we wished to approach the exercise and what issues we wished to address. Out of this developed a working group consisting of five people who met over a three-and-a-half year period. Each member of the group, myself included, took responsibility for one major topic. I also spent time with each of them individually, assisting them to formulate a theological perspective on their chosen theme.

Throughout that period, we met monthly over an extended lunch hour or for an after-work session so that all could share what they were doing. During those times we also worked our way through certain materials and issues relevant to the whole project. For example, we looked at a number of biblical figures who were involved in administration and at a number of other passages relevant to our concerns. We also examined writings by professional theologians and by people in the field of public administration that bore on the issues we were considering. Towards the end of times together we also developed a number of case studies around the topics on which we were working.

Every nine months or so the working group presented its findings to a larger group of public servants. This in turn led to further research and discussion by the initial group. Some of the members made visits to other capital cities to enlarge their understanding of the factors involved at the state rather than federal level. At a later stage the group invited two others who had investigated adjacent areas of interest to contribute to its work. Finally, it organised a national conference of federal and state public servants, augmented by representatives from other interested groups. Following this it produced a book containing all the major contributions, together with resource materials, in the hope that this would help other groups to form and wrestle with similar problems.[4]

----

4. See further R. Banks (ed.), *Private Values and Public Policy: the Ethics of Decision-making in Government Administration*, Anzea, 1983, especially the introduction which describes the process followed.

This type of working group could be duplicated among members of many other occupations and professions. There are few fields of employment where Christians are carrying out serious work of this kind, despite the growing interest in the ethical dimensions of their faith. However, here and there groups are at work in similar ways. I know of some among economists, social workers, psychologists and accountants. Sometimes their concerns are less highly focussed than in the group I have described and not everyone takes responsibility for working at a particular issue. Although in part they have the character of study groups, of which more in a moment, they do contain some features of the model I have outlined.

A related approach to exploring industrial issues has been developed by the Department of Mission at Selly Oak College in Birmingham, England. This separates out the role of facilitator and theological consultant and includes certain other ways of proceeding. The following are laid down to be followed :

(a) The group itself rather than the resource person decides which of the issues raised by members will be investigated and agrees on a basic method of approach. The presenter of the situation-study then provides more detail, but remains silent till the group reconstructs it and re-presents it for checking. At any point in this process members may suggest a different direction or call attention to extra factors.

(b) The group's 'knowing', as established by their common work, now becomes the basis for what follows. While it can ask the presenter of the issue for more detail, at some point the members cannot ask for any more information. This matches the real life situation in which people often have to deal with problems with inadequate information.

(c) The main features of the development of the situation-study are elaborated on and listed on a board. This includes pinpointing the pressures falling on people, the major powers at work and the human consequences. Then some search is made for one or two 'handles' on the situation so that a practical way into the problem can be opened up.

(d) The next step is to identify the policies being pursued by the principal parties, assess the world views and value judgments that underlie these policies and develop a theological critique of these views and values.

(e) At this point it may be helpful to call in some theological experts, who might also provide help with more general questions deserving attention that the group has unearthed.

(f) From this point on there is a search for an alternative theological basis for dealing with the situation, a delineation of policies which might be developed from this basis and the testing of such policies for realism, particularly by persons who will be involved in implementing them.

(g) By now the group has developed a strong sense of community and members are in a position to offer personal support to any of their number who is having to cope with the situation.[5]

working group approach is an effective way of exploring subjects other than professional or industrial matters. For example, if you are a member of a special interest or single issue group, in addition to any research and discussion you are already doing it is simply a matter of finding other Christians with the same concern who would be interested in developing a more explicit Christian understanding. More everyday, even routine activities could also be pursued in a similar way: all that you would need is a certain degree of shared experience, a willingness to stay with the group until the work is done and access to a person who has some theological expertise combined with a sensitivity to everyday issues.

You might approach some of these matters by enrolling in a course of study or joining a study group, but for many issues you would find this less helpful. Few aspects of everyday life have been explored adequately from a Christian

---

5. I. Fraser, *Reinventing Theology as People's Work*, USPG, pp.61-65

point of view for anyone to teach them effectively or prepare resource materials for study group use. In any case, a course of study can only give a second-hand appreciation of the issues. It cannot really match the more concrete learning that takes place through belonging to a working group.

However, sometimes it is difficult to find other people to form a working group around a particular subject. In a particular congregation, place of employment or special interest group, there may not be sufficient people with the same concerns or enough time. If this is the case, contacting a Christian resource centre or lay education institute may put you in touch with others who have similar interests. If this fails to provide what you are looking for, or at the present you do not have the time to give to a working group, then a study group or course, if such exists, may have to do for the present.

The power of participatory thinking

Over the last two decades the workshop has become a familiar part of the adult education scene. The difference between a working group and a workshop is partly a matter of numbers and partly a function of time. Whereas a working group normally involves only a few people, a workshop can encompass a larger number. A working group generally continues over a period of time, whereas a workshop is a briefer, more intensive affair.

Although workshops have been part of the Christian scene for a while, there is still a tendency to favour the seminar or conference as a context for learning. Even where workshops are available on a variety of topics, there seems to be little attempt to develop a pattern of integrated learning around them. Workshops are mostly one-off functions. There is also an inclination to use workshops for less demanding subjects. For that reason many people feel, wrongly in my view, that they are not a suitable vehicle for dealing with complex issues.

Workshops certainly provide an excellent way of grappling

with a wide range of practical dilemmas. As an example, consider the issue of busyness and the pressure of time. When
I first began to be invited to speak on this subject I tended
to tackle it alone in a highly instructional way. But increasingly I have moved in a more workshop direction and involve
others with me as resource persons. We have found that a
workshop on this topic is most effective when it takes place
over an extended period of time; that is, intensively over a
weekend or less intensively over a week or fortnight.

We attempt to find out at the very beginning where those
attending it are in relation to the time issue. Each group is
different and it is important for us to find out how they are
affected by this pressure. One way of discovering this is to
encourage everyone to engage in personal reflection for a
period of time, writing down what comes to mind and then
sharing it, if they wish, with the group as a whole. Once we
have learned where members of the group are in relation to
the time issue, we know whether we have to restructure
what we have planned and give more attention to some
matters than others.

Turning the whole group into a workshop also enables the
participants to discover for themselves the main factors
which quicken the pace of life and engender busyness. This
also enables them to 'own' their own responsibility in the
matter as well as 'disown' factors over which they have no
control. My role in that process is simply to ask the right
kinds of questions and to group the responses in an instruc-
tive way, in this case distinguishing between the way our
goals, values, drives, circumstances and inadequacies affect
our approach to time.

If the group has its attention drawn to the most important
biblical passages dealing with time, it is able to begin
developing its own Christian perspective on the problem.
This is best done by dividing it into discussion groups and
asking them to report their findings when they come back
together. We have found that there is no need for directive
questions about the passages for study. Groups unearth for

themselves the basic principles which should affect their attitude to time and use of it. My contribution is then to order
these and expand on them where it is helpful to do so.

At the close of the time, after we have shared some of the
ways we have begun to overcome the pressures of time, we
invite others to share with the whole group any helpful hints
which they have discovered for themselves. This procedure
tends to be less prescriptive and threatening as well as more
practical and diverse than other ways of recommending a
solution. Finally everyone is asked to spend some time
quietly listing a few concrete steps they can take to reduce
the degree of busyness in their lives. They are encouraged
to resolve prayerfully with God to do something about these
in the coming week.

I have gone into some detail here in order to convey some
sense of the way in which any group of Christians with a
modicum of help from a well-prepared resource person can
workshop its way through to its own conclusions. As a learning experience this is far more effective than heavy doses of
instruction from the front, even where this contains incisive
sociological analysis, biblical exposition and detailed application. This kind of instruction tends to evaporate soon after
the session is over whereas what people have analysed,
worked out and decided for themselves is much more likely
to stay with them. It is far easier for the resource person to
have a high profile and do almost everything up front. It is
much harder to design such a workshop, discern when and
how it must be varied while it is in process, and co-ordinate
individual or group responses in a way that does most justice
to them.

But the workshop approach is not only suited to practical
matters. I have also used it extensively in apologetic work
with small groups of 'doubters'. We begin by hearing their
stories about how they came to their present views. The
issues that emerge form the 'curriculum' of the remaining
meetings as we deal with one person's central doubt each
week. This approach keeps these issues close to the every-

day experiences which often generated them, ensuring that they are not discussed in a purely cerebral way.

With respect to vocational ethics, workshops based upon case studies are an excellent way of opening up problem areas. The case study approach is widely used in management schools and administrative training and is also being introduced into formal theological education. One of the difficulties is that good case studies arise out of a long process themselves. They do not come easily, even when built upon the experiences of those who are formulating them, and it is the prior efforts of a working group that often stands behind them.

The respected Christian educationalist Thomas Groome also emphasises the value of workshops. He has tested these out on a wide range of groups in a wide variety of settings. In his book *Christian Religious Education: Sharing our Story and Vision*, he explains what he calls his 'shared praxis' approach:

> Over the past years I have used a shared praxis approach with adults and high school and grade school students (in both school and parish contexts), in weekend retreats, seminars, symposia, conventions, community renewal and team training programs, and so on. Gradually, from both apparent successes and failures, five recognisable pedagogical movements have emerged. . . .
>
> i. the participants are invited to name their own activity concerning the topic for attention (present action);
>
> ii. they are invited to reflect on why they do what they do, and what the likely or intended consequences of their action are (criticial reflection);
>
> iii. the educator presents to the group the Christian story concerning the topic at hand and the faith response it invites (story and its vision);
>
> iv. the participants are invited to appropriate the story to their lives in a dialogue with their own stories (dialectic between story and stories);
>
> v. there is an opportunity to choose a personal faith

response for the future (dialectic between vision and visions).

There is really nothing sacred about the number five, and other educators may find it helpful to adjust, combine or increase the movements.[6]

Workshops certainly could be used in many current learning contexts such as annual camps, houseparties or conferences. Where they do take place in these settings, they tend to be on the margins not at the centre of the program. One writer has said the following about what happens when experts and addresses dominate these gatherings:

> . . . all that is left to the whole body of people is to react, posi-
> tively or negatively, to what has been presented to them. The
> more brilliant the speaker is, the less they are free to think
> their own thoughts and make their own contribution. The
> alternative is to replace keynote speakers with resource
> persons; and plan preparation to find out what, in their situa-
> tion, participants are facing or should be facing. Agreed
> homework is then done in anticipation. . . it is those who
> have done this homework who are the catalysts. They share
> and check theological insights, working in small groups and
> then in plenary; identify pastoral responsibilities; commit
> themselves to forms of action; and, using their own words,
> draw into worship the longings, discoveries and rejoicings
> which had surfaced over the time of encounter. The specialist
> gives the people confidence that the work is properly theirs,
> helps the process to develop so that they make the most of
> what is theirs and of what is given them by others, and is
> ready to intervene to add some theological reflections or
> question some findings.[7]

As those of you who have been involved extensively in well-organised workshops know, the workshop approach to learn-

---

6. T. Groome, *Christian Religious Education: Sharing our Story and Vision*, Harper and Row, 1980, pp.157-162
7. I. Fraser, op.cit., p.39

ing has many advantages. It engages us more fully than traditional modes of teaching so that we absorb more of what is being discussed. It develops our capacity to listen to and learn from one another and so brings out into the open the underlying perceptions and feelings that shape our attitudes. It draws on a wider range of insights and experience and therefore encourages both more subtle and more specific learning to take place.

The key to good workshops is a group who share a common concern and at least one resource person willing to assist. Sometimes you will find such a group and person in a congregation or other Christian organisation. Alternatively, a resource centre or lay education institute may put you in touch with other people who have similar concerns and with someone who can provide some resources.

Several heads are better than one

Study groups which meet in a work environment or around a common concern also have their place. In the past, Christian occupational groups have tended to operate mainly for a devotional purpose or to provide fellowship for their members. Only rarely have such groups or the annual conferences which sometimes bring their members together focussed on their work situation and the institutions to which they belong. During the last two decades study groups have begun to develop more around a range of moral and social issues. On some of these issues resources are available from denominational, para-church or secular groups. As yet, however, study groups have given less attention to more everyday matters and their dynamics sometimes hinder their members learning in a holistic way.

In his book *Working Out Your Own Beliefs: A Guide for Doing Your Own Theology*, Douglas Wingeier makes a number of useful suggestions which members of study groups wishing to develop a personal theology might employ, both in preparation for the group and when it meets. Preparing for the group may involve general reflection, focussed meditation and journal writing. He begins by proposing that you write down an important decision you made recently. This should include something about the background, alternative choices involved, and factors supporting or opposing these. Then add how you felt during or after the decision, what values you said yes or no to in deciding the way you did things, what God was trying to say to you through the process, and in what ways your decision is consistent with the biblical message, church teachings, your ideals or previous experience of God's guidance.

He suggests various ways of building on this in the group meeting. For example, each person in the group could list the ten values they affirm most strongly or five goals they most wish to accomplish. Then everyone chooses the two values and goals that most guide their behaviour, share these with someone whose values and goals are not too dissimilar and finally debrief as a group, voicing feeling, learnings, needs and common goals. Focussed prayers similar to those mentioned above could conclude the gathering. This exercise, he says, helps people to begin making the connection between faith and life.

Since he defines 'doing theology' as 'reflecting on experience from the stance of faith, making use of the resources of scripture and Christian tradition', Wingeier then offers four pairs of exercises for private and group use, similar in style to the above, focussing in turn on learning from experience, reason, scripture and tradition. So in the next time of private preparation, we should concentrate on and write about an experience rather than a decision. The accompanying time of group reflection could centre on sharing or discussing this. Alternatively, it could involve imaginatively entering into a biblical story and then talking about how it affected us, or choosing a biblical term that identifies something in us and asking what experience led us to use this and what simile we might prefer to put in its place, again sharing our reflections with the group.

In the following weeks individual preparation focusses on

a key turning point in life, next a meaningful Bible passage and finally a film, book, event or scripture. He suggests we seek to interpret these, identifying feelings and images associated with them, discerning the presence of God and responding to what is learned both practically and prayerfully. The corresponding group exercises involve:

(a) portraying or diagramming a key turning point in our lives and allowing discussion to focus on the world view reflected in the story that explains it, the role of conscience in what takes place and the self-image involved;

(b) finding a particular character, parable, image or event in the Bible with which we can identify and reflecting on the good news, encouragement or challenge in the story;

(c) selecting a central phrase from the creed, checking out its scriptural basis and traditional meaning and asking how far it is a vital part of our own experience and shaping factor in our lives.[8]

Wingeier's approach moves out from everyday experience and draws on the Bible to correct and extend that. In my view the role of the Bible could have been emphasised more. But it is also possible to begin with the Bible first and move out into everyday experience. In England, John Davies has developed a useful approach to Bible-study that keeps it in touch with ordinary concerns. He describes this as follows:

We take time off from our ordinary programme of life; we pick up the Bible; we read a passage, say, which describes an event in the activity of Jesus.' The first thing we must do, is establish connections with our immediate experience. Relevant questions are:

☐ What does the story connect with in our experience?

☐ What bells does it ring in our memory?

☐ What little details in the story interest us? Why?

☐ Are there any problems for us in the story?

☐ What character can we identify with?

☐ Would we like to be the teller of the story? Why?

---

8. D.E. Wingeier, op.cit., 1980

Having read the event in its original context more thoroughly, further questions can then be asked. For example:

☐ Do we see anything interesting about the place which the story has in the gospel?

☐ Why do we think the evangelist was interested in the story?

☐ Why do we think that Christians in the early church were interested in the story?

Finally, the group turns back to the present. Relevant questions now are:

☐ What message or mandate do we get from the story:
for ourselves?...
for our disciple group?...
for our neighbourhood?...
for our country?...
for the world?

☐ Who or what is being commended in the story in contemporary terms?

☐ Who or what is being criticised?

☐ What new attitudes are encouraged?

☐ What new action is suggested for the disciple-community today?[9]

Group members then go back to their ordinary program of life. This approach has some similarities with that developed by Walter Wink in the United States.

A further approach to Bible-study is the so-called 'narrative exegesis' one. Weaving biblical materials into a story rather than argument is a very fruitful way of bringing people into touch with what the Bible says. Not only does the story format enable them to enter more fully into and discover more fully for themselves what the Bible contains. Such a story triggers people's own stories about similar incidents, occasions, questions and concerns and this enables a greater interaction to take place between God's revelation

9. Quoted in I. Fraser, op.cit., pp.56-60. For a related approach see W.Wink, *Transforming Bible Study*, SCM, 1980

and our present situation. Both Walter Hollenweger and Hans Reudi-Weber have developed materials along this line, and my own *Going to Church in the First Century* is similar in character.[10]

Study groups require access to helpful resources if they are to work effectively. This may come through a member of the group. While such a person may have some familiarity with academic theology, this is not strictly necessary. Alternatively, discussion group material may be provided by an outside institution. In this case, all the group needs is a good facilitator. A good facilitator is more important than a leader; that is, one who claims to know what is best for the group and controls its operation. The presence of a leader in this sense, or of an expert in theology, is more of a hindrance than a help unless this person is willing to have a low profile and act as a resource person.

The value of properly formed study groups is evident. Since they depend upon each member making a contribution, they increase the possibility of a better grasp of the matter they are discussing. They provide a context in which a variety of everyday issues can come up for inspection. But such groups function best when they are not just forums for exchanging ideas but to some degree supportive fellowships as well. Only when this element is present will members feel free to talk about some of their significant interests and concerns. Where these groups take place in the actual environment in which the issue arises there is an extra edge to their deliberations.

Where formal learning fits in

Where do formal courses of study fit into all this? There are two dangers to be avoided here. On the one hand some people feel that gaining a Christian perspective on the business of day-to-day living is incompatible with academic

---

10. See R. Banks, *Going to Church in the First Century*, 2nd.ed., Hexagon, 1985

study. They would argue that turning it into a program of formal study takes it out of the everyday dimension and turns it into something more rarefied. But this only reinforces the view that the everyday dimension of life is secondary and not worth thinking about very much. On the other hand, some people assume that developing a theology of ordinary life can only take place in an institutional setting through extensive programs of study. But full-time study in such a setting will only be possible for a small proportion of people. Also, formal study can only bridge the gap between belief and life at the level of thinking: it does not of itself ensure the right kind of character formation that empowers people to translate ideas into action.

Still, attending formal courses has some role to play in integrating belief and life. At some point in their lives, many Christians would benefit from the systematic thinking such study encourages. They will benefit most from this after they have had some experience in the world, so that they come to it having already formulated some questions and can test what they hear from the wisdom they have already accumulated. But what kind of content should such a program have? It should have a different starting-point from the typical curriculum in a theological college.

An excellent example of what can be done is the interdisciplinary, team-taught, faculty-attended, Ministry of the Laity course at New College, Berkeley. Over a semester this course identifies all the main areas of life that require thoughtful Christian consideration and helps people to do this in a preliminary way. Areas covered include: *The Vision: renewal in mind and life, Biblical studies for the laity, Historical and cross-cultural studies for the laity, Theological and ethical studies for the laity, Integrative studies and practical experience, Lay spirituality, Laity in the church, Lay people in society and cultture, Laity in workplace and marketplace.* Such a course opens up most of the relevant issues and lays a firm basis for any future study.

In Canberra over the last two years we have piloted two

courses of study which give the average Christian a grasp of what is in the biblical writings and what is their Christian heritage. These courses, which run over a year each, are designed for groups of around eight people, including a facilitator. The first, the biblical overview, involves reading about twenty-five chapters of the Bible a week, keeping a daily summary of what is covered and meeting weekly for around two to three hours to share insights. This is not done with a view to gaining some systematic doctrinal or ethical understanding of what the Bible contains. Nor is it a guided tour in the sense that everyone is provided with set questions to which they must find answers from each set of readings.

There is a three-fold aim: to help those taking part to gain an overall grasp of the biblical drama or story as part of the biography of God, to trace a practical theme of their own choosing through the Bible, and to be alert to points where God's story touches their own. The method is highly participatory: it is an invitation to self-discovery and mutual sharing in which participants dwell on what strikes them from their readings — what excites them, puzzles them, troubles them, challenges them — rather than attempting to discuss every passage read or tie up every thread set loose. The enthusiasm generated by this way of approaching the Bible and its impact upon thinking and behaviour has been nothing less than phenomenal.

We have followed this with a similar ten-month-long exercise introducing Christians to aspects of their 'family tree'. This Christian heritage course differs from conventional courses in church history in a number of ways. So far as the content is concerned, it focusses on key, life-giving movements and figures rather than endeavouring to give a blow-by-blow description of all that has happened. It looks not only at religious leaders and at ecclesiastical developments but at Christians who had a significant influence upon other areas of life such as social structures, law and injustice, science, politics, education, music and literature, family life and spirituality. Throughout there is an eye to what these movements and figures have to say to us now in our twentieth-century situation. As far as method is concerned, once again each person reads material in preparation for the week's meeting. Each one also takes responsibility for investigating and presenting the life of four key figures throughout the year. There is a facilitator who has some general knowledge of the whole area or who has done the course already.

Both the biblical overview and Christian heritage courses train people as they undertake them to facilitate a group later themselves. Although not everyone will have the capacity to do this, each group should be able to produce one or two people who can do so. This means that the courses are self-reproducing and do not require the presence of an expert or theologically trained person within them. While recourse to such a person may be helpful from time to time they are not needed on a week-by-week basis.

After completing the kinds of courses I have mentioned, if you wished to pursue further formal study, you might move in any one of a number of directions. In the biblical area, there could be a study of various everyday concerns — Jesus' attitude to such issues as work, leisure, morality, race, and politics. Sections of the biblical writings that especially impinge upon everyday life, such as the wisdom literature in the Old Testament and practical portions in the New, are also important. So far as history is concerned, attention could be given to the Christian interface with a particular aspect of intellectual, social or cultural life. Some examples are: the contribution of 'lay' theologians to a Christian understanding of society, the influence of Christian ideas and practice upon social welfare, and the development of modern music, painting or literature from a Christian perspective.

In systematics, certain doctrines such as creation and providence, the kingdom of God, vocation and the covenant are extremely relevant to everyday life issues. But then such central concerns as the incarnation, cross, resurrection and eschatology also have significant implications in this area. I will say more about this in the final chapter. In drawing on the views of past Christian thinkers and leaders, a workshop approach can sometimes be extremely effective. Different members of the class can take the part of different sides to the debate as well as represent the views of contemporary religious groups who hold some of the same views. This enables them to get inside the positions adopted instead of looking at them from a distance.

With regard to ethics, there is a large range of questions you might explore: the ethics of sex, family and the single life; moral, social and political issues; professional and occupational concerns; our responsibility to the suburb, city and the environment. It is possible to create an agenda around the particular ethical questions which people bring with them; indeed, these can provide the basis around which a whole course is run. Where other issues come up for consideration, far more can be gained from a case-study approach than a conventional lecture format.

The more the formal courses of study are geared around the particular concerns which people bring with them, the more the traditional divisions between theological disciplines begin to fall away. It is questionable how far these should govern appointments and courses in institutions orientated to the average Christian, for when a particular dilemma, interest, issue or occupation is the chief focus of concern, we ought to bring every theological discipline to bear upon it. This means that inter-disciplinary work will be the norm rather than the exception in any considered Christian approach to everyday life. So, too, will a new type of teacher, trained in some theological discipline perhaps, be more a skilful general practitioner than a specialist.

A concluding clarification

Throughout this chapter I have indicated the wide range of ways in which we can develop a Christian approach to everyday life. At a number of points I have also emphasised the difference between these and conventional approaches to

Christian and theological education. I would not wish to leave the impression that a theology by, for and of the people is somehow less demanding than the other or inferior to it. John Macquarrie has stated the matter well:

> It cannot be asserted too strongly that lay theology is not, so to speak, theology made easy, a simplified or abridged version of a 'professional' theology. Although in ordinary usage the word 'lay' is often contrasted with 'professional', it does not have that sense here... A lay theology might well dispense with some of the jargon, though theology will always need some technical words for accuracy of expression. But a lay theology is not an easy version of an academic theology, and it would be an insult to the intelligence of the layman to suggest that it is. All theology demands hard thinking. Lay theology is not a simplified version of academic theology but rather a corrective to it, broadening its base and bringing into being a theology that is more representative of the whole Christian community.[11]

If the theological education of ordinary Christians omits or only touches some parts of the traditional theological curriculum, it is because such items are less relevant, not because they are too difficult. The same rigour of thought that is required of those training for ordination — detailed attention to historico- critical methods, to the fine points of ecclesiastical doctrine or to the subtleties of denominational relationships — must be applied to everyday life issues that concern the average Christian. These include the complexities of decision-making, the ambiguities of life in the public arena and the distinctives of a genuinely Christian lifestyle. I am not suggesting that all Christians should reflect on such matters in the same way, to the same degree or at the same level. But we must recognise that the dilemmas most Christians confront are often as intricate, subtle and perplexing as those that fill traditional theological textbooks.

---

11. John Macquarrie, op.cit., p.4

5

A people's theology

IF THE FIRST STEP in developing a Christian perspective on all the business of life is finding an appropriate learning context, what happens next? By what means do we learn how to bridge the gap between biblical statements and the different, sometimes more complex situations we encounter today? How much can secular knowledge help us formulate a Christian response? Is there a distinctively Christian outlook on all everyday dilemmas? What is the role of those with formal theological qualifications in this process? Should certain matters have priority over others? In order to do justice to these issues, I will have to speak more specificially to professional theologians than I have done to this point.

Every person a theologian

I believe a theology of everyday life works best when all Christians, not just professional theologians, are involved in it. Let us examine this under four main headings:

1. *Ordinary Christians can best identify their everyday concerns.* I have already discussed my involvement with a working group of senior public servants. The members of this group were searching for ways in which they could bring their private values and public responsibilities into greater harmony.[1] Our first task was to identify their dilemmas more

---

1. Also on this topic see J. Haughey (ed.), *Personal Values in Public Policy: Conversations on Government Decision-making*, Paulist, 1979

precisely. Over the initial three-month period, meeting fort-
nightly, my task was simply to listen, ask questions and list
the concerns they were expressing. At the end of this time,
I helped them to categorise six main problem areas within
which several types of difficulties arose. With this list in
hand, there was further discussion about which matters
should receive first consideration. This partly depended on
what they saw as the most significant problems for them per-
sonally and what problems they felt they had most compe-
tence in tackling. From the list, four matters were eventually
chosen as provisional topics.

This was not the end of the agenda-setting process. After
members of the group had given preliminary consideration to
these four topics, we arranged several further meetings with
a wider range of public servants. It was up to this group to
decide whether the four chosen problems-areas provided the
best starting-point and whether they were being approached
in the most fruitful way. Only at the end of this second series
of meetings was it resolved to go ahead and explore the four
issues in depth.

I learned far more from this stage of the process than I contributed. But for this to happen I had to leave behind certain
attitudes programmed into me by my professional theological training. If you have had this training, you are tempted
to think that you are the one to identify the issues which are
important. In any case, professional theologians suffer from
certain disadvantages in this whole area. The first has to do
with the context in which most of them work. Bruce Wilson
puts this well:

> Perhaps the most significant change which the so-called
> process of secularisation has brought to the modern church is
> the split in our consciousness, in our society, in our culture
> between the sacred and the secular. It is a split which enters
> into the life of our churches too. The laity, as we call them,
> live, and more importantly work, in that zone of occupation
> loosely called secular. The clergy, as we call them, live, work

and experience most of their face-to-face relationships in the zone of the sacred. And whatever we call them, academic theologians or lecturers in theology mostly live, work and have their being in academised ecclesias or ecclesiased academies.[2]

In other words, the professional theologian and the average Christian do not, in many respects, inhabit the same mental world. Though this is not true of all those who have undergone formal theological training, it is true of many such people. In most cases, theologians are ordained and work in ecclesiastical institutions. Their training and ethos set them at two removes from the majority of Christians. Of course, some theologians are not ordained and work in an academic setting. To some extent this enables them to escape what Bruce Wilson terms the 'priestified theology' that often emerges from theological institutions. But these theologians frequently fall prey to an 'academicised theology' that only relates to an educated elite.

If you are a professional theologian, you might well object that you do after all carry on part of your life outside the ecclesiastical or academic domain. Like everyone else you read a newspaper in the morning and put out the garbage at night. You raise a family, look after a home, wash the car, work in the garden and play sport like everyone else. In any case, do not many of the same problems that arise in other professions and settings invade the church and university as well? All this is true, but two problems remain.

If you work in an ecclesiastical context, this will tend to colour what you see as important and not. Theologians often reside in a kind of ecclesiastical compound, especially when they live and teach in the same environment, and this bears a little of the same relationship to the outside world as did mission compounds in foreign cities. I say 'a little' because

---

2. B. Wilson,'Notes Towards a Theology of Everyday Life' in *St Mark's Review*, 126, 1986, p.17

I do not want to press the analogy too far. But many people who are not professional theologians do comment on the artificial flavour of so much theological conversation.

In addition, professional theologians only have access to some of the everyday concerns other Christians have. There are many that still lie outside the theologian's experience and these can only be explored in the company of a wider group of people. While books can sometimes help you get some feeling for these concerns and the context in which they arise, these do not cover every situation either and are rarely a substitute for contact with people involved in the situation itself. This is why the gap between academic theology and everyday life cannot be closed by people who live much of the time on the 'sacred' side of the line determining what lies on the 'secular' side. On their own such people can only guess what lies across the border.

2. *Ordinary Christians already have some elements*
of an everyday theology.

Over the last few years I have had intermittent contact with a group of Christian economists. The group is a diverse one, with a mixture of people from the business world, university circles and government administration. The group has been in existence a number of years. It meets every six weeks or so in the office of one of its members. While some group discussions centre on books or articles recommended by one of the members or on a talk given by someone from outside, others stem from papers prepared by one of those present. Some of these papers have been collected and made available for distribution. The group has even arranged a small conference which drew together economists from two other capital cities.

Last year I was asked to give a theological response to a paper that had been discussed at the previous meeting. Its presenter, who worked in a government department, was challenging the existing economic model that guided government farming policy in Australia. The paper questioned a number of widespread economic assumptions, raised the question of values in a provocative way and argued for the relevance of a religiously based social vision to policy formation.

I opened my remarks by saying that I was not going to give a theological response to the paper so much as make explicit the theological dimension that already existed in it, as well as elaborating on this by reference to insights from biblical and ethical studies. It was obvious that the integrity with which the presenter had been wrestling with rural policy in his work and the experience he had gained over many years as a working economist had enabled him to develop a thoughtful and fundamentally Christian approach to this area. Though he was not aware of many biblical and professional theological resources that might bear on the issue, he did have an intuitive feeling for them. In this way he was becoming what I like to term a de facto theologian with respect to his vocation.

I have to stress this in the face of another temptation for professional theologians. For even if these acknowledge the role of other Christians in drawing up an agenda of everyday concerns, they might assume that they are the ones to formulate the theological response to those concerns. Such theologians sometimes betray their attitude here by speaking about the importance of fashioning a theology *for*, and perhaps even *of*, the people of God, without recognising that this must be a theology *by* the people of God as well. At this point a paternalistic note can all too easily insert itself. Professional theologians also display a paternalistic attitude when they think instinctively of providing courses on matters arising out of the ongoing business of life. In so doing they reveal their belief that they have or can find the answers to the questions the average Christian is asking.

This outlook is at odds with the authentic spirit of Christianity. While certain people undoubtedly have a responsibility to draw out the implications of the gospel in a more subtle and systematic way than others, all Christians are capable of doing this in some measure and in some areas only they can do this. As the Australian theologian Graham Hughes writes:

> This is to suggest that there will be an infinite gradation in levels of discernment at which the task of theology will be carried out. The man who sits down in his farmhouse kitchen with an open Bible, the educated housewife preparing to lead a senior Bible class group, the minister in his study or the professor in his library are obviously all working at very different levels and with very different audiences in view. What I want to say is that there is no essential difference in *what* they are doing, provided they are properly about their job. They are all trying to understand what God is saying to us today. They are all busy about the task of theology.[3]

Theology, therefore, is not only an academic subject for brighter Christians or for those who wish to become ordained.

We need to go further. Even Graham Hughes' examples of ordinary people doing theology are too orientated to forms of learning that involve study. What, for example, about learning that comes through insight? This kind of learning is not so much something we give ourselves to as something that is given to us. It is born out of attending to God in meditation and prayer. It is born out of attending to the created order and intuiting messages from it. It is born out of attending to life and receiving parables from it. Attentive waiting, wonder and listening are the midwife of insight. And when insight is set beside insight, and there is an attempt to interpret and connect them, theology is in the making.

Learning also comes through careful observation. The processes of nature, its patterns and rhythms, can teach us a great deal about the character of God and the nature of everyday life. Other people's behaviour can instruct us in a whole range of ways about how to behave or not behave,

---

3. G. Hughes, 'Every Man a Theologian', *Interchange*, 18, 1976, p.121

what causes and flows from certain kinds of actions, which choices, possibilities and alternatives exist when we have to make decisions. Observing these leads to understanding of a different kind to insight. One is deductive, the other inductive. One is won, the other given. Yet both have their source in God. Both these ways of learning can affect us unconsciously. But when we become aware of them and reflect on them we are engaging in theological understanding.

Learning also takes place through personal experience.[4] It is not only as we study the Bible, hear a sermon or read a religious book that we grow in Christian understanding nor only as we observe the way others, structures and nature works. Anyone who is reflecting Christianly in a serious and ordered way about their paid employment, childraising or favourite sport is in the business of doing theology. In the examples I have given, such people are attempting to fashion from their experience a theology of vocation, marriage and leisure respectively, in the hope that it will guide their daily living. Not that this is always a highly rational and systematic affair or something that only revolves around problems and decisions. Much of it flows spontaneously from the kind of person each is becoming and relates to any aspect of what each is engaged in.

Since many Christians are learning in all these ways, we should take encouragement from it. For it means that the general absence of a Christian understanding of everyday life at the public level does not mean it is altogether absent in the private sphere. In many instances the starting points and some of the directions are already there. The problem is that they have not been recognised as such or articulated enough. The first task is to bring to the surface those intentions, motives, dispositions and principles which already guide the attitudes and actions of the kinds of Christians I have men-

---

4. See further the preface to my book, *Paul's Idea of Community: The Early Home Churches in their Historical Setting*, Anzea, 1979 and Eerdmans, 1987

tioned. Many of these starting points and directions may have inadequacies. Some may need to be discarded. Most will need to be developed. Most benefit from evaluation from appropriate people outside the setting in which they were developed. All will require scrutiny in the light of Bible teaching. But they are the basic building blocks of any theology of everyday life and it is with them that we must begin.

3. *Everyday theology is a co-operative effort between ordinary Christians and professional theologians.*

In preparing to write a book on the tyranny of time in modern life, I learned much from a broad range of people about the difficulties they had with time and the questions these provoked. I also learned that some individuals, families and groups had discovered ways of coping with the problem of time or creatively dealing with it. Only as I worked through the material with these and other groups was I able to gain further insight into the problem. I made it my business to raise the matter in conversation whenever I had opportunity to do so. I sought out occasions where I could share what I was thinking in greater depth. I was able to do this in a variety of contexts: day seminars, weekend conferences, week-long units and semester courses; and with audiences as diverse as students, teachers, public servants, politicians, minorities, academics and missionaries, as well as many heterogeneous groups of Christians.

I gained a great deal from these discussions. Some of the comments made opened up new perspectives which I had not thought about. Some of the ideas I advocated were challenged. Several times I was provided with practical recommendations for dealing with the pressures of time. As a result of encouraging people to respond to these sessions in other than purely verbal ways, I was offered songs, hymns, stories, parables, cartoons and prayers which crystallised people's feelings about our wrestling with the issue. In many respects, then, my work on the problem of time and the book which came out of it was a corporate effort, a mosaic of contributions from a wide range of Christians. Whatever value it has owes much to this.

If as a professional theologian you wish to deal with the business of everyday life, you cannot simply sit down in your study and — with the help of biblical, theological and other relevant writings — provide what is needed. You must involve a wide range of Christians in the process. They are not simply there to frame the questions and suggest some of the ingredients. They have a fundamental role to play in developing both the theoretical and practical understanding of the issue. This is even more clearly the case when the matter under discussion is not one with which you are familiar but distinctive to their own situation. There are two steps to consider here.

First, those who have had direct exposure to the issue at hand have a greater understanding of the situation. Others may look in from the outside and discern something of what is involved. Because of their detachment they may even see certain things more clearly. But those who are closest to the heart of any issue do have access to all kinds of information — technical, practical and perhaps even theoretical — which is essential to any informed response. Admittedly, some of this information can be gleaned from reports and statistics, from academic studies and from fictional accounts of similar situations. But it is rare for these sources to provide the sharp definition of an issue that comes from someone on the scene. As Jurgen Moltmann is fond of saying to theological students in his courses on Christian Ethics: when a doctrinal dispute emerges in the church you are the experts. But when an ethical dilemma arises in secular life, it is Christians touched by it who are the experts, not you. In such matters, you are not the professionals and they the lay people; you are the lay people and they the professionals.

Second, Christians who have some stake in the issue under discussion are able to interpret theologically the information they have to bring to it. It is through the give and take of discussion that the most significant factors for an issue become apparent. It is by the same means that a Christian perspective on it comes into sharper focus, each helping the other to go beyond the de facto theological insights they already possess. This takes time, for understanding in depth rarely comes quickly. It takes even longer to work out effective recommendations for action. It is at this point that so many reports or statements emanating from church bodies are at their weakest. Such bodies tend to have too many 'experts' and not enough grassroots representatives. Without the participation of a wide variety of people — from all kinds of class and ethnic backgrounds, with all types of educational and practical qualifications, and in all sorts of work and non-work situations — a fully-rounded and thoroughly relevant theology of everyday life will not come into existence.

4. *A workable theology of everyday life requires*
   practical testing by ordinary Christians.

Over many years those involved in the home churches with whom we have had contact have felt that they would like to share their experiences with a wider audience. In the first instance, this centred on talking about what we had discovered with interested congregations and para-church organisations. But there was also the thought that at some time it would be appropriate for us to put our thoughts on paper. Now and again we were encouraged by a publisher to do this. But for a long time neither we nor others in our groups felt that we had learned enough to do this.

Consequently, apart from two or three general articles, it was more than fifteen years after our groups had begun that the moment to write something substantial seemed right. To have written anything on the subject before that would have been premature. Not that we felt when the moment came that we had fully 'arrived'. Far from it. But at least the model had been tested sufficiently to put it before others with some confidence. The book that resulted was in large measure a communal exercise, gathering together the contributions of people in a variety of home churches, jointly edited and written by my wife and myself. Only so, we felt, would the book capture some of the real flavour and diversity of home church life.[5]

Unfortunately thinking and learning in the West tends to take place chiefly *for* rather than *through* practice. Theory comes first and application follows. We learn now in order to act later. In this way we separate, at times even invert, processes that are commonplace in other cultures. Undoubtedly our approach has many virtues: our extraordinary scientific and technological development bears witness to that. But it has also generated problems for which we do not as yet have answers. In fact, our impotence partly stems from the way we bring the very same faculties to bear on remedying problems that created those situations in the first place. We persist in thinking that we can always work out solutions in the abstract instead of realising that they will only emerge as thinking and action interact and modify one another.

Christian thinking over the last few centuries has largely succumbed to this approach. In this matter we have been more shaped by our culture than we realise. We also tend to concentrate on learning *for* rather than *through* action. From Sunday school lessons, through Bible-study groups and into theological education our minds are filled with information for future use. While some of this is valuable, even necessary, too much of it creates a dangerous divorce between thought and behaviour, doctrine and life. For our most significant learning takes place through a subtler yet more practical process. It takes place through the constant interplay of reflection and action, each orientated towards the other. While there is a place for more general instruction that is not closely related to behaviour, this is secondary. I do not wish to devalue its importance, but it is not what changes people or society. As someone has said: 'the problem with most Christian pedagogy (sermons, theological lectures etc.) is

---

5. R. and J. Banks, op.cit., 1989

that its primary purpose is *information* rather than *transformation*.'[6]

Yet the Bible endorses the more dynamic approach to learning and the lives of many major Christian pioneers and thinkers illustrate it. The meaning of the word 'know' in the Bible, often commented upon by theologians but rarely influencing the way they teach, binds understanding and doing inextricably together. To 'know' is not merely to understand what God has said, nor is it to do what you understand. For you only show that you understand by doing and it is in the doing that understanding partly comes.

Paul exemplifies this: his profound theological insights did not come to him overnight, nor did they drop out of the blue. It was mainly through coming to terms with personal suffering and social humiliation, and through engaging with problems his congregations were encountering, that his understanding developed. In large measure this was also true of such people as Augustine, Luther and Calvin. Attention recently has been given to the centrality of the idea of 'relevance' in Calvin's writings and it was this that gave the consistently practical cast to the best of Puritan preaching and writing. If any group of Christians took seriously the importance of relating their systematic beliefs to all the business of life it was the Puritans. While the more extreme oppressive effects of some of this have lingered long in Western consciousness, any close reading of the leading Puritans demonstrates how much concern there was to relate theology to everyday concerns in a vital and balanced way. Wesley continued this tradition as did several of the earliest evangelicals such as Wilberforce, who himself wrote on the need for what he termed 'a reformation of manners'. Significant strands in the thought of such figures as Kierkegaard and Bonhoeffer also possess this character. In all these people thinking and acting shaped and informed one another.

---

6. N. Carr, 'The Social Impact of Christian Theology and Pedagogy', *The Journal of Christian Education*, 86, 1986, p.24

Reflection was directed towards life and was also influenced by it. This is why so much of what they wrote remains vital and relevant today.

A Christian understanding of all the business of life must possess something of the same spirit. If it is forged in the cut and thrust of everyday life it will also have vitality and relevance. The best person to implement and judge the value of any Christian approach to everyday situations is the average Christian. But it takes time to do this and the process must not be hurried. If it is short-circuited through the desire for quick results, whatever comes out of it will not be adequate. Only if it is given its proper time will the real benefits appear. Whatever emerges will then have a sharper cutting edge and become a genuine force for change.

If a Christian theology of everyday life allows its agenda to arise from the concrete dilemmas that ordinary people confront, if it builds on the best features of the rudimentary theology that some Christians have already developed, if it arises from discussion involving a wide range of people wrestling with a common problem and if it is also tested by such people for its practical value, it will have much to offer.

Theology of the whole person

1. Towards a holistic approach to life

I would not wish to give the impression that developing a Christian approach to all the business of life only involves serious thought or detailed recommendations. We are constantly in danger of over-stressing the role of the intellect in our lives. We are also vulnerable to developing casuistic regulations to guide our behaviour. If we succumb to the first danger we have fallen into the Greek temptation that Paul inveighs so strongly against in his letters to the Corinthians. If we succumb to the second we have fallen into the Pharisaic temptation that Jesus attacked so consistently throughout his ministry.

First, we are more than thinking machines. There is a rationality of the emotions, imagination and will as much as of the intellect. Only when we are developing in all these areas will we live fully integrated Christian lives. Only as we are becoming mature in our feelings and intuitions, discovering the most powerful and penetrating images for viewing reality, and strengthening our ability to commit ourselves to difficult courses of action will we become and do what we want. Relying on the rationality of our intellects alone will not take us far enough.

For example, our basic thinking is done through images not propositions, though propositions flow from these images, and only if our imaginations are being renewed will our thinking follow suit. As Richard Broholm says, 'many of the values and beliefs we hold are expressed through images and... these images largely govern our behaviour. To change one's behaviour involves changing the images that instruct and reinforce that behaviour ...'[7] That is why the Bible speaks to us so often through images — God as father, Christ's death as a sacrifice, the church as a body, the Christian life as a walk, heaven as a city.

Similarly, unless our emotions are being trained alongside our intellects, then our lives will not reflect the passionate, deeply-felt side of God revealed to us in the prophetic and apostolic writings, but only his thoughts. We will think and act like computers, lacking not just the feelings to go with our attitudes, but the sensitivity which helps us discern what is appropriate behaviour anyway. And what use would it be to know how to think about and negotiate everyday life if we did not have the power to live that out? In itself broadening and deepening our understanding does not necessarily lead to changes in our behaviour and unless we are becoming more empowered as well as more knowledgeable we are not changing in any fundamental way.

This means assisting Christians to develop the right kind

7. R. Broholm, 'Envisioning and Equipping the Saints for Change', *The Laity in Ministry: The Whole People of God for the Whole World*, G. Peck and J.S. Hoffman (eds.), pp.131-133

of character as well as the right kinds of ideas. If all a theology for everyday life produces is a series of principles and recommendations, it will have fallen into the same trap as the casuistic books on ethics written for earlier generations of Catholics and Protestants. Such principles and recommendations have their place. But as well we need potent images, symbols and models to stimulate our thinking and behaviour. We also need freedom and flexibility to intuit what we should do in situations which are untypical or in which more than one option is valid. We do not always need to have detailed regulations at hand in order to live responsibly.

There is another problem with the casuistic approach to life. Practical though some of the older manuals were, often they lacked vitality. They did not give life so much as constrain it. They failed to realise that our actions are fundamentally a function of our character. I am not suggesting that if only we attend to forming character we will automatically do what is right. That would be the opposite, pietistic error. Our character develops as we become increasingly aware of the complexity of life and wrestle with specific decisions we have to make. It also develops as we connect up the various parts of our lives into an integrated whole and have some sense of where we have come from, where we are now and where we are heading. Having a sense of our own 'story' and gaining a feeling for others' 'stories' is also necessary if we are to act rightly.

Most basic of all is a real familiarity with God's 'story' as revealed in the Bible. The Bible is only secondarily a source of doctrine and ethics, of beliefs and principles; primarily it is 'the greatest story ever told' and as such it has the profoundest impact upon the individual 'stories' we write for our own lives, right down to the most everyday level.[8]

---

8. See especially here the work of S. Hauerwas, *A Community of Character: toward a Constructive Christian Social Ethic*, University of Notre Dame, 1981 and, with particular reference to the theme of their book, James D. Anderson and E.E. Jones, *Ministry of the Laity*, Harper and Row, 1986.

If character plays a vital part in our ability to act Christianly in everyday situations, we cannot overlook the importance of those contexts which most helpfully shape it. Here I can only stress the central — and mutually dependent — place that both relating to God and relating to others must have in our lives. Unless I am clearing time for God to show himself to me and love me, to reveal his dreams for me and deepen my affection for him, to talk to and with me, and to empower me through the wide range of ways he makes his Spirit available to me, I will never get very far in developing an integrated Christian life. And unless I am in a real relationship with a small group of fellow Christians, opening myself up to them and learning how to love them, sharing my dreams with them and growing in sensitivity to them, reflecting on what God is saying and open to their correcting, I will only get so far but no further. In fact, so dependent are these two ways of relating on one another, that I cannot even get very far with either one unless I am deeply involved in both. This is as true for the professional theologian as for anyone else.[9]

But both relating to God and relating to others — piety and community — must be inextricably intertwined with the everyday world in which we live, not escapes from it or havens in it. Our spirituality should not only touch our so-called inner life — which in any case is significantly shaped by all that we do and experience in our day-to-day affairs — but emerge through and connect with the complex web of situations, incidents and encounters that make up our lives. It, too, should have an everyday cast to it: we should constantly be meeting God *in* it, not only *apart* from it. Through intimations, parables and dreams as well as through what we hear, read and observe, the voice of God, which as the Psalmist reminds us is never silent, should echo in our minds.

Our communal life with other Christians should also have its feet on the ground. Gathering with them ought not

---

9. See especially Parker J. Palmer, op.cit., chapters 3 and 7

revolve around so-called spiritual concerns alone, but embrace every aspect of our lives. It is as whole people that we must relate to one another and church ought be the place we show any of our concerns — in the home, at work, to do with our leisure, within our neighbourhood, relating to our society at large. These are the matters with which the scriptures should be brought into contact and which should become the subject of prayer, whatever else might be important for us to share with God and one another.

2. Integrating doctrine and ethics

Some of you might wonder whether the high profile I have given to ethical and other practical concerns is due to my devaluing the importance of doctrine. This is not so. What I am arguing for is the reconciliation of ethics and doctrine. They have been divorced too long and the separation is unbiblical. In the legal and prophetic writings in the Old Testament and in the teaching of Jesus and Paul in the New, doctrine and ethics are a seamless whole.

In fact, one could argue that what we call ethics predominates.[10] One is never discussed for long without reference to the other. It is we who have divided them and placed them in different compartments. This gap between doctrine and ethics is one of the reasons that we have failed to develop a satisfactory theology of everyday life. All key doctrines have their practical dimension just as all practical matters have their doctrinal aspect.

This being the case, we can only tackle many everyday issues by investigating basic Christian doctrines more deeply. For example:

□The doctrine of *creation* speaks to us of the dynamic activity of God in the world. It does this not only in general terms, but talks specifically about the quality of God's creative work and his concern for detail. The Bible establishes a

---

10. A new work affirming the fundamental place of ethics for doctrine is J.W. McClendon Jr. *Systematic Theology: Ethics*, Abingdon, 1986

connection between God's creativity and ours and between his work and our work. It alerts us to the need for a balance between work and rest as well as between production and appreciation. It affirms our trusteeship for the environment and of our mandate to develop it responsibly. Creation also embraces the role of and our relationship with the animal kingdom.

☐One of the most neglected doctrines is that of *providence*. If it does come into discussion it is mostly in connection with God's general supervision of history or with the problem of suffering and evil. But the main theme of this teaching is his preservation of, care for and involvement in the human, animal and material world, at the structural as well as individual level. We can only make sense of many of our more everyday activities, ranging from routine matters like housework to interests like gardening or keeping pets, along with much of the voluntary and paid work that we do, if we view it within the framework of God's providence.

☐The whole business of life is the forum for working out our Christian responsibility, not just what happens in our individual, family or church affairs.

* In the past, Protestants developed a doctrine of *vocation* to express this conviction. This affirms all Christians as ministers of Christ, not only in the church but in the world, an idea that must be broadened to include other responsibilities like raising a family and other activities such as those we now refer to as avocations.

* Those inclined in a more Catholic direction placed greater emphasis upon the *incarnation*. This underlines our need to take the world seriously and not downgrade its importance and the importance of full identification with those in it, particularly with those who are disadvantaged in any way.

* In the present more emphasis has been laid on the idea of *liberation*. Here we are reminded of the possibility of change in social, economic and political structures as well as personal life.

All these have some part to play in developing a theology of everyday life, but there is an even more fundamental place for the central doctrines of the *cross and resurrection* of Christ. While these may seem somewhat removed from the realities of the workplace or of everyday routine, in fact they are not. The cross and resurrection remind us of God's inversion of this world's values and of the way in which this should influence our motives, choices and behaviour. There is a direct line between these central realities of the Christian faith and notions of servant-leadership or transformation of the ordinary. And we should not forget the cosmic relevance of the cross and resurrection: their hidden impact upon the whole created and supernatural order.[11]

□*Justification* is one of the central biblical doctrines. In the past this has been upheld against attempts to circumvent it by a false emphasis on justification by works. Sometimes these works have taken the form of moral regulations, as with the Pharisees in the time of Jesus, or of ritual obligations, as with many Catholics in the time of Luther. But nowadays people tend to justify their lives — whether to others, themselves or God — primarily through their secular work or job. This is the main form that justification by works takes today and it is present within the church as well as outside it, even within the ordained ministry. The idolatry of work in modern life can only be dealt a mortal blow by means of a redirected doctrine of justification by faith.

□In fact, there is a vital place for a proper understanding of *idolatry* and of the role of the *principalities and powers*. With few exceptions there has been a singular lack of application of the idea of idolatry in Christian analyses of contemporary life. This is less true of the biblical teaching on principalities and powers, though often these have simply been identified with ideologies and social structures. We cannot understand the power, both constructive and destructive, of the pres-

---

11. See P. Marshall, 'Dying and Rising with Christ: Theology for a Modern World', *Zadok papers*, Series 2, 1986

sures, traditions, institutions and preoccupations in our society without looking at them through these biblical categories.

☐The idea of the *covenant* is significant in thinking about our responsibility and accountability to others. This has reference to a number of areas in life. It is relevant to the work situation, especially with respect to promises, obligations and contracts. In the spheres of friendship and marriage it provides the basis and informs the character of the relationships entered into. In regard to society at large the notion of covenant plays a central part in the formation and dynamics of voluntary associations.

☐A fully-developed theology of the *Spirit* should recognise the rich potential and extraordinary diversity of the capacities God has given us. It would speak of the abilities given to people through the general activity of the Spirit in the world and with the Spirit's special presence in the church. The nature and exercise of power are also illumined through study of the Spirit's character and ways of operating. The significance of the group as a context for exercising any type of gift is also important.

☐An appreciation of *eschatology* is also fundamental. This may seem surprising for do not everyday concerns by definition have to do with this life not the next? But we cannot separate the two, as Paul for one reminds us forcibly in 1 Corinthians 7. Everyday situations and responsibilities must be lived in the light of the eternal dimension; the quality of life in the latter throws light upon the norms that should characterise life in this world; the presence of hope and willingness to take the long-term view are also firmly rooted in our awareness and experience of heavenly realities.

It is not easy to translate such doctrinal convictions into practical recommendations. We can only do this if we take some intermediate steps which bridge the gap between the biblical world and our own. What form should those intermediate steps take? Some encourage us to frame 'moral presumptions', which are what we might call the ethical 'bottom line' from which our thinking should begin and the ethical 'outer boundary' beyond which we cannot go. While no simple deductions can be made from these as to what we should do, they create room for a range of valid, changing and even conflicting possibilities for action. Others talk about the need for 'action-orientated principles' which are immediate implications of biblical principles that can be put into practical effect without further modification. These are applicable to any age, though general in character and requiring more detail to provide concrete guidance.

Still others favour the use of 'operative norms'. These are more specific, vary from one age or culture to another, yet still fall short of detailed policies or plans. Not all Christians are likely to agree to these. Finally, there are those who refer to the value of 'middle axioms'. These seek to maintain the highest level of agreement between Christians from a number of viewpoints while allowing them to be implemented in a variety of ways. To some extent these approaches are complementary, to some extent they are alternatives. I do not wish to evaluate them here, but simply emphasise the need for some kind of intermediate steps if we are to produce a biblically-based but practically relevant Christian understanding of everyday life.

3. The value and limits of specialist resources

Where do specialist theological resources come in and who should be the one to investigate them? Let me discuss the resources first. Naturally you will want to draw on any biblical and theological studies that are relevant. But you will probably find that such studies are limited in value. The works of biblical scholars are useful for identifying many of the biblical passages relevant to everyday concerns, for giving the meaning of key images and concepts and for providing signposts suggesting the general direction from which solutions may come. Newer socio-historical and sociological approaches to the Bible are valuable where they yield a clearer understanding of everyday life in biblical times, making it easier to discern the differences and similitaries with our situation today.

But both older and newer style biblical studies rarely take up contemporary issues and, even where they do, tend to do this in a practical way. They also pay less attention to some materials that may be relevant to such issues. So when dealing with an everyday concern someone will have extra biblical work to do and will also have to work harder at applying it to the matter at hand. Whoever does this will find it rewarding to dwell on the wisdom materials in both the Old and New Testament. This material is often closest to many of the concerns of the average Christian. Its neglect is one of the reasons for the gap between belief and daily life. Although we must not consider the wisdom writings independently of other parts of the Bible, such as the prophetic writings and apostolic letters, they are often a helpful starting point for the consideration of everyday concerns.

I have found the work of systematic theologians to be as much frustrating as helpful. Once it ranges beyond central doctrinal concerns which, though they often could be, are not frequently linked to everyday issues, it tends to concentrate on philosophical or perhaps broader social or cultural issues. The latter can be quite interesting and at times form a background to the consideration of more everyday concerns. But in my experience it is only now and again, and generally in the writings of the leading theologians, that everyday concerns occasionally come into view. The writings of the great Danish thinker of the last century, Soren Kierkegaard, or of Karl Barth, the most famous theologian of this century, contain some marvellous flashes of insight into everyday problems.

Writings in Christian ethics are also helpful for the suggestions they make about the best methods of approach and for the light they throw on some current ethical dilemmas. But with some fine exceptions, they tend to set out the biblical perspective on first-century issues without dealing with their contemporary application or deal with a limited number of contemporary issues without doing justice to the biblical data. Increasingly, there seems to be a concern to bring the Bible and contemporary problems together, but there is still a long way to go. And such writings mainly focus on problems, overlooking other aspects of life which are less problems than just part and parcel of life.

In dealing with issues of everyday life it is important to consult materials from a wide range of other disciplines, such as history, literature, psychology, economics and sociology, as well as from such areas as urban, media, managerial and administrative studies. Whenever these are likely to throw light on the issue under discussion, they should be investigated. So, too, should more wide-ranging works on the history of ideas or behaviour along with informed analyses of present cultural attitudes, forces and trends. As well as providing valuable information about the world in which we live, these works at times contain pointers to or expressions of God's truth. That is, they have picked up traces of his general revelation. Too much theological reflection depends upon the Bible or 'special revelation' alone and does not take sufficient account of other sources of knowledge. That is why it often seems remote from ordinary life. It is essential to test material from these other sources for false presuppositions, data and interpretations, and to see how much or little of it is consonant with a biblical framework. But to overlook it is to miss some of the clues God has left lying about for solving the puzzles that daily confront us.

Also not to be overlooked are popular or semi-popular writings which dissect a slice of contemporary life, synthesise insights from diverse academic fields or present an individual response to our current way of life. Some of these do not have a great deal of sophistication. But at times they are more down-to-earth and perceptive than weightier discussions. Also relevant are non-literary areas such as popular music, contemporary film and newspaper cartoons. It also embraces popular Christian writings. Now and again these show more insight than scholars' learned treatises. Sometimes the 'foolishness' of those with less formal theological education is wiser than the 'wisdom' of their more professionally qualified counterparts.

4. A new paradigm for theology

Who should have the responsibility of drawing in the specialist resources I have mentioned? Someone who has some formal training in theology would find it easiest to discover what is available and make most sense of it. But only if certain other factors are present. For example, such a person must be familiar not only with theological resources but with other specialist resources as well, otherwise there will be too narrow a perspective. It would be possible for someone else to identify non-theological resources that were available. This would present no problem so long as the two specialists could work together fruitfully. This points up the need for a quite different capacity.

The professional theologian must have some relational as well as intellectual skills. Otherwise there will be no genuine co-operation even with other specialists, quite apart from other Christians involved in the process. In fact, the professional theologian must be prepared to be a servant to others in the group. This is another area where the notion of 'servant' or 'enabling' leadership must be present. If the professional assumes control over the group or allows specialist resources to overwhelm the empirical experience others bring to it, very little of worth will emerge.

You will contribute most to such an exercise if you are seeking to develop a theological perspective on your own daily activities. It is easier to integrate your thinking and actions at this point than in areas of life with which you are less familiar. This was so for me with respect to the issue of time. It had arisen as a personal problem long before I began thinking systematically about it. I had already gained some basic insights into it and tested out some possible solutions before I began writing on it.

Our life with God, in meditation and prayer, is also vital here. For ultimately what we are looking for is a divine perspective upon these activities. Meditation enables us to perceive what lies in and through phenomena as opposed to merely looking at these with our eyes or our minds. We begin to see things as they really are, not just as they appear. We begin to view matters through God's eyes, not just at a nice objective distance. We begin to feel passionately about things, not just form conclusions about them. As Lionel Thornton says, becoming a genuinely practical theologian involves not only 'human understanding, intuitive insights and spiritual perception as well as learning', but also 'prayer as mediator within the total theological scheme... In this wide, deep sense prayer is the total experience of all things in Christ.' Indeed, the intuitions and hunches which guide research and begin to provide answers 'are unlikely to arise except under the influence of prayer'. Also, detailed studies do not always lead to 'a Q.E.D. solution to the problem, but at least to a personal hypothesis, or even a paradox, which can be made subject to contemplation'.[12]. A theology of everyday life that has insight and power must have a decidedly autobiographical and contemplative character.[13]

In addition we need 'full-time' theologians who have at least one foot firmly planted in the world. If you sense some vocation in this area, you could delay equipping yourself in a more formal sense until after you have experienced and reflected more on your work, family and community involvement on which you have already reflected. If you are already involved professionally in theological work, you might step out from it for an extended period and work in a secular and non-academic environment, perhaps even in some cases coming to see this as your permanent location. Or, as occa-

12. M. Thornton, op.cit., pp.69, 72
13. The theologian who has most used an autobiographical approach is Harvey Cox. See, for example, his book on *The Seduction of the Spirit: The Use and Abuse of People's Religion*, Simon and Schuster, 1973

sionally happens, you might combine part-time theological teaching with part-time but substantial involvement with people in serious need, as takes place with base communities in Latin America. Any of these moves would bring invaluable 'qualifications' that no academic credentials can provide.

If you plan to study theology at an advanced level you could consider diverging from the usual research directions and format. As Lionel Thornton notes:

> Our modern divinity faculties swarm with research students the results of whose studies will never be published and in many cases will never be read. I hopefully suggest that they would be better employed doing pastoral theology, regarded as an equal but separate discipline from scholarship. The results of such studies, demanding every bit as much intellectual application plus spiritual and imaginative insight, would I believe stand up better to the essential qualification for any worthy thesis: that of original thought.[14]

Certainly the outcome of such work would be deeply appreciated by many more Christians, especially if you drew their dilemmas, experience and wisdom into your research. There are scores of everyday issues which as yet have received little or no formal theological scrutiny. Of course, it is not only research students but their teachers who need to revise their research and writing priorities.

Apart from the occasional non-technical book or denominational report, academic theologians more often write for their peers or their students than for the average Christian. Even their more popular efforts tend in both form and content to be dilutions of their more technical works. There are other forms of communication, such as dialogue, narrative, autobiography, as well as letters, parables and workbooks. But how much have these been used? Having tried my hand at some of these in a small way I know how difficult it is. But we need

---

14. M. Thornton, op.cit., p.123

writings of this kind and, as the work of C.S. Lewis and others demonstrates, if it is done well, they will be widely read.

But these proposals only refashion the current image of the theologian. What I said earlier about the fundamental role of images for our thinking has a particular application here. We need a new image of theology, not just a more informed and relevant theology, if we are to develop an effective understanding of everyday life.[15] We also need a new image of what it means to be a theologian. Democratising theology so that it becomes the province of a larger population of Christians who are prepared to think about their faith in a coherent way is one aspect of this. But we need a new image of the 'full-time' theologian as well. This is a vocation that some have. But from what I have said already it is clear that academic credentials are no longer enough to qualify a person for this responsibility. As well as democratising of theology we need a deprofessionalising of the theologian as well. This takes us further than any suggestions I have made so far.

We need 'apostolic' theologians who will leave their desk and lectern for a more down-to-earth kind of life. While there are few theologians who do not practise what they preach in some measure, there are very few who are engaged in similar work, say, to someone like Paul. That is, in apologetic and evangelistic work, in church-planting and pastoring, in pioneering new models of education and training. The apostolic theologian, of which Paul was the first great exponent, places mission first and largely allows theological reflection to be generated by that. Learning goes on as people associate with him or her in that activity — observing, questioning and imitating. There is no reason why many Christians cannot be involved with such a person and why many of their concerns cannot be dealt with in this setting.

---

15. E. Farley, *Theologia: The Fragmentation and Unity of Theological Education*, Fortress, 1983 and M. Stackhouse, *Apologia: Contextualisation, Globalisation and Mission in Theological Education*, Eerdmans, 1988

The trouble is that taking up the 'apostolic' theological life entails a large drop in status and high degree of risk.

We also need a large number of what I like to term 'bare-foot' theologians. This is where those of you who are not professional theologians come back into the centre of the picture. In many Third World countries there are insufficient doctors to cope with demands for medical help. Those trained to fill this gap have only an elementary medical training. Yet such people have been able to treat some eighty percent of the illnesses they confront. In a different area, Wycliffe Bible Translators have for decades successfully taken non-linguistically qualified people and given them the basic skills for translating the Bible into another language. I cannot think of any reason why the same principle cannot be followed in the theological area. All that is required is some familiarity with the major types of issues that might arise and certain skills in assisting others to work through those issues. Some of you are already relatively well self-trained in the theological area. Others have some formal theological education. Much of the knowledge many theologians have gained, and other experiences they have had, is underemployed. Given some additional practical training, which would best come from someone who can model for them what they might do, they would be well placed to help other Christians develop a theology of everyday life. In fact, my guess is that the future of such a theology largely lies in their hands.

If we are to encourage a larger number of people to become 'apostolic' or 'barefoot' theologians, we cannot leave it to present theological institutions to produce them. Some of these institutions are beginning to break out of the traditional model of theological education, but they are still largely committed to it. Lay theological centres, most of which significantly have developed outside the main theological structures, are better placed to help, but many of them are also too influenced by the dominant model. Theological education by extension programmes have some possibilities for overcoming the barrier, but these are still geared mainly to church-related ministries and emphasise some aspects of the learning process more than others. In addition to what all these can do, we require contemporary versions of the more practically-orientated and holistic 'Paul-Timothy' type of theological training. Of themselves these may not be enough, but without them something vital will be lacking.

Conclusion

So then the call to develop a theology of everyday life is in the long run a call to develop a new understanding and practice of theology itself. It is not just a call for theology to broaden its concerns, for theologians to enter a new field or for theological colleges to fill out their curricula. Ultimately, it is a call to everyone involved in these to re-examine the model they are following and transform it into another. It is a call for a new form of theology and for new forms through which it may be expressed.

Nor is it just a plea to all Christians to become more aware of their dilemmas and responsibilities, to think more about the implications of their faith, to belong to more study groups and attend more courses. It is, fundamentally, a plea to re-examine what it means to be a Christian. It is a plea to develop a new vision and total style of life through which the reality of God may be expressed.

---

16. Though he is addressing the issue of Christian education more generally, helpful clues to the way learning should take place in such training may be found in Parker J. Palmer, *To Know As We Are Known: A Spirituality of Education*, Harper & Row, 1983

Appendix A:

Lay theology and education since 1945

OVER THE LAST FEW DECADES there has been a number of attempts to relate theology more closely to the world at the level of both ideas and practice. How far do these attempts take us into the everyday life of the average Christian? To the extent that they do, and do so effectively, we can build on them. I have made no effort to be exhaustive here, but rather sought to identify the main approaches. I have singled out three representative books, each of which came to my attention at an appropriate point in my own thinking or work. I have also discussed a number of representative institutions I have visited which attempt to take theology to a wider audience.

The first steps

From the Second World War onwards there was a growing interest in what was termed 'the role of the laity' in both the church and the world. Some of this interest stemmed from gatherings, reports and groups of the World Council of Churches. According to Hans Reudi-Weber, there were many reasons for this discovery:

> It is partly due to the biblical and theological renewal which has revealed to us a new image of the church : the church as a people and a body, the church which is elected and sent for mission and service in God's world. The rediscovery also partly stems from our new world situation: the breakdown of

the corpus Christianum; the processes of industrialisation and secularisation which tend to edge the church out of daily life into a religious ghetto; the fact that the church is becoming almost everywhere a minority which has great difficulty in communicating with the modern world. Wherever these new insights about the nature and task of the church and these challenges of the modern world are taken seriously — and the ecumenical movement attempts to do so — the question of the role of the laity immediately becomes prominent.[1]

During the same period, various major denominations were also rediscovering the importance of the laity. This was true in Catholic as well as Protestant circles.[2] In part this was for similar reasons. But these denominations, and the congregations of which they were composed, felt some of the factors noted by Hans Reudi-Weber more directly. Some pastors and evangelists began to see the potential in their church members and devised ways of training them to be more effectively involved in congregational life. I can still remember the novelty of hearing about the courses and openings for church members set up by people like John Stott in England. Or the programmes and responsibilities arranged for Christians who were counsellors at Billy Graham evangelistic crusades. Later the influence of fresh religious impulses upon the denominations led to greater involvement on the part of many church members. In the wake of the charismatic movement this was true in the exercise of so-called spiritual gifts. Meanwhile the radical discipleship movement led to a renewed interest in serving the community and confronting social and political issues. Local churches and denominations were also more directly aware of the declining numbers of people attending church and this

1. H.-R.Weber, 'The Rediscovery of the Laity in the Ecumenical Movement', *The Layman in Christian History*, S. Neill and H.-R.Weber (eds.), SCM, 1963, pp.379-380
2. Y. Congar, *Lay people in the Church: A Study for a Theology of the Laity*, Chapman, 2nd.ed., 1964

led to a variety of suggestions for mobilising them or attracting them back to the fold. These ranged from new organisations within the congregation to full-scale stewarship schemes. Lay representation was also increased on denominational committees, conferences and working groups and there was a larger provision of chaplains to Christians in industry, universities and other institutions.

This new mood was powerfully captured in a book published in 1958 by the well-known ecumenical missiologist, Hendrik Kraemer, entitled *A Theology of the Laity*.[3] This occasioned a great deal of interest and was reprinted several times in the next few years. In no other writing during that period was the role of the average Christian in both church and world argued so strongly and thoughtfully. I did not come across this book until some six or seven years after it was published. At that stage I was having increasing difficulties with the existence and consequences of the clergy/lay distinction in the church at large and was beginning to question the preoccupation in most local churches with filling their own buildings and organisations rather than encouraging their members to fulfil their responsibilities as Christians in the wider community. When I finally got round to opening the book, I did not so much read it as devour it. It helped me realise just how introverted and onesided most churches were and how much I myself had contributed to that. I could see how much they prevented those same people from fully playing their part in the world as well.

In his book, Kraemer stressed the centrality of the lay person both in the church and in the world and pleaded that fuller theological attention be given to this. He insisted that the role of the laity in both spheres had been regarded merely as an appendix to the doctrine of the church. Or, in the development of a Christian view of society, it had been treated too generally. He asked that the term 'laity' include more than the elite non-clerical members of the church. It

3. H. Kraemer, *The Theology of the Laity*, Lutterworth, 1958

should embrace women and men, poor and wealthy, less-educated and well-educated, working class and middle class. What was required was not just a theology of, but also for, the laity. To be effective, this had to be free from the technicalities of professional theology. It would only develop, he pointed out, through the co-operation of theologians and lay people.

According to Kraemer, nothing less was required than a reversal in priorities. God's primary concern is for the world, not the church, and the church should reflect this in its own life. Although the church often claims that it exists on behalf of the world, in practice it is a highly introverted institution. The church must not only have missions or give service to the world, but become inherently a missionary and servant body. Christ embodied these two concerns in his own life and every lay person is required to imitate him. This is not a matter of following an ethical example, but entering into a new way of life involving the whole person. Such a calling is as real as that of a missionary or an ordained minister and is in no way inferior to them. Here, said Kraemer, we have the starting point for a theology of the laity. He did not claim to be saying anything new; merely placing at the the centre of the doctrine and structures of the church something that till now had been relegated to the periphery.

Kraemer concluded that two major changes had to take place if a theology of the laity were to genuinely emerge. First, there must be a thoroughgoing revision of church structures. This includes the development of new forms of community such as house churches, in which the laity can really become the church. The laity must also have a greater share in preaching and leading worship at larger services. The church's activities must also be decentralised to cope with the mobility and diversity of modern life. Second, there should be a relocation of the place where dialogue between the church and the world occurs. Instead of this happening in church councils at a distance from the issues discussed, it should take place at existing meeting points where ordinary people work, live and play. For it is through the laity, dispersed in the world, that this dialogue is already under way. If this dialogue is to be properly informed, it needs prayerful support, pastoral encouragement and theological assistance.

For Kraemer also there was an indispensable complement to a theology of the laity. We needed 'various theologies of the realities and spheres of the world', such as those of work, money, property, common life, and a personal and social ethics which addressed these issues.[4] Listening carefully to the world so that a genuine encounter with it takes place was crucial here. Only so would we discover the hidden points in the world which are the levers for social change. Actually contributing to the life of the world would express itself in a variety of ways, such as being certain kinds of people, undertaking disinterested service, becoming reconcilers in volatile conflicts, asking the hard questions which no one else is raising, and prophetically contradicting the world where necessary.

As I read this book I had a sense of mounting enthusiasm and challenge. So much has been written on this subject since, and so much of what Kraemer said has been taken for granted, that it is hard for me to recapture the freshness of the book's impact. But indicators of that impact are there in the book as I look at it again. Halfway through reading it I began to underline large sections of the text. Then I began to put ticks, write comments and insert exclamations in the margin. The ticks multiplied and the comments became more and more affirmative the further I read. By these means I can retrace the upward curve of my excitement.

Kraemer's book crystallised the concerns underlying the formation of various institutions in Europe after the Second World War, beginning with the Evangelical Academy at Bad Boll in West Germany. These institutions sought to give lay people a theological understanding of their responsibilities in church and world and to equip them better for service in

---

4. H. Kraemer, op. cit., p.185

both. Unlike seminaries and Bible schools, they focussed mainly on people in secular employment and addressed issues relevant to their workaday lives. The academies also developed short, intensive courses of various kinds rather than full-time study programmes.

My first encounter with one of these institutions was in the winter of 1968. I was studying in Switzerland at the time and a German friend took me to to the Evangelical Academy at Mannedorf, not far from where we were living. This was quite unlike any institution I had visited in my own country. It had something of the atmosphere of a Christian conference centre, yet was clearly a place where serious study and research took place. It was also frequented by many people who were not attenders of any church. The visit broadened my understanding of what could be done to assist Christians to relate their faith to life generally and to enhance the interchange between church and world.

The majority of these centres emerged in Western Europe. This was no accident, for the ravages of the Second World War left much to be done in the area of moral and social reconstruction. Many people, irrespective of their attitude to religion, wanted their societies to rebuild on a sound foundation. This was especially the case in Germany. Though these centres grew out of a particular social situation and took different forms in different countries, there was an underlying similarity in their goals, structures and approaches.[5]

The evangelical academies in Germany from 1945 onwards saw themselves as centres for discussion and research. Initially they drew together politicians, jurists, church administrators and employees into two-week conferences so that they could discuss their specific concerns. In the following years conferences diversified. There were specific gatherings for different kinds of workers — appren-

---

5. On these and other possibilities for lay education made during this period see M. Gibbs and T.R. Morton, *God's Lively People: Christians in Tomorrow's World*, Fontana, 1971.

tices, master craftsmen, people in commerce, engineers, secretaries and industrial leaders. Later on, attempts were made to bring all the different types of workers and levels of management in a single firm together. Operating through, and partly subsidised by industry and government, the academies issued their invitations to everyone in these groups, irrespective of their involvement in a church. The continuing State Church pattern in Germany aided this approach.

The academies also established special services to particular occupational groups. One such service attempted to draw teachers in elementary and secondary schools into conversation with church officials. Another concerned itself with labour questions and sought to create Christian cells in industry, form local workers' study groups, establish links between churches and labour and make contact with the unions. The academies also developed links with other groups such as farmers. As well, there were courses for students wishing to enter journalism and conferences for editors at which religious, social and cultural questions were discussed in the light of the gospel. The academies also realised that some matters required more thorough study than was possible through these channels. This led to the creation of a network of university teachers who could contribute their expertise on particular issues. Questions discussed ranged from the role of Marxism in contemporary thought and life to social and vocational aspects of the life of the working woman.

In other parts of Europe centres developed that had much in common with the evangelical academies, but also differed from them. For example, the Iona Community in Scotland, composed of both ordained and non-ordained people united in a community of worship and work, grew out of the life of an intentional community. The Ecumenical Institute in Bossey, Switzerland, sprang from the desire to draw lay people and their concerns more fully into the work of the World Council of Churches. The Kerk in Werld movement in Holland set up a distinct sociological institute and established a centre to equip church workers through non-formal training. Other organisations were set up in Sigtuna, Sweden, in Mannedorf, Switzerland and, with some difficulty, in various parts of the German Democratic Republic. In time, Catholic centres developed in some of these countries. Here and there co-operation between Catholic and Protestant institutions also took place.

Unfortunately, the reliance upon academic resource people in many of these centres has tended to undermine their relevance and has also increased the expense involved in running them. Too great a reliance upon government subsidies has also at times interfered with the direction of their work. The emergence of independent, more specialised ministries to Christians in the workforce is also forcing these institutions to redefine their goals and activities. Most recently, cutbacks in government aid are requiring them to rationalise their operations and close some of their centres. So far as I can gather, they have also tended to focus increasingly upon ministers and churchgoers rather than aiming at broader participation.

It was not until later that organisations sharing some of the concerns of these centres arose outside Europe. These organisations have tended to lack the broad financial and secular backing that the European centres possessed and are less diverse in their operations. Ones with which I have had varying degrees of personal contact include the Zadok Centre in Canberra, Australia, the Shaftesbury Project in Nottingham, England, and the Centre for the Study of Ethics and Social Policy, Berkeley, USA. All of them are committed to developing a theology of the laity along the lines advocated by Kraemer. They provide resources for groups who wish to integrate faith and life. From time to time they hold workshops, seminars and conferences for people in different occupations or who are concerned about particular issues. They also encourage the formation of vocational and other groups to think through such matters. Of course these are not the only institutions engaged in such activities, but they are among the most committed to it.

Some new developments

During the last fifteen years there have been some interesting developments in the area of what is described as 'lay theology'. Among books written on the issue is one by Richard Mouw entitled *Called to Holy Worldliness*.[6] This was written towards the end of the seventies out of its author's experience of many debates on the issue of lay responsibility to the gospel. Someone drew my attention to this book a couple of years after it was published. At the time I was deeply involved in the working-group, seminars and conference for senior government administrators that I have already mentioned. This exercise had been under way for three years and was nearing its completion. But we were encountering real difficulty in persuading the wider body of Christians in the Public Service of the basis upon which our whole endeavour rested — that their faith should impinge in some way upon the actual work they were doing and the institution in which they were doing it. In order to address this prior issue, we began to search around for material that would convince them, preferably by a lay person who would talk more in their own language.

It was at this point that we came across the book by Richard Mouw. What is particularly interesting about the book is the way it embodies the main shifts in emphasis that had taken place in developing a theology of the laity since the publication of Kraemer's book just over twenty years before. For example, Mouw's background is the Christian college rather than the seminary scene and a chief interest in social ethics. Being also an educator, he is able to bridge the gap between the worlds of the theologian and the average person. Mouw was also conscious of the need to go 'beyond Kraemer' and views his work as forming 'chapter two' of a

---

6. R. Mouw, *Called to Holy Wordliness*, Fortress, 1980

theology of the laity. Therefore he begins at the point at which Kraemer's book ends, that is he simply assumes that lay people should take their full position in the church, develop a theological perspective upon their role in society, and find new ways of structuring and carrying out their responsibilities. He wishes to go further and be more specific about what a theology of the laity entails.

Mouw begins by noting the gap that still exists between theology and the corporate life of society — business, politics, education and entertainment. He finds a similar gap between the concern for piety or evangelism on the one hand and the reality of social structures on the other. He does not regard the bridging of this gap as the only concern of lay people and does not regard all lay people as equally obligated to do something about it. But he does stress the need for more lay people to become involved in this area. Although in his view the situation has improved since Kraemar wrote, there is still a need for extensive discussion of the role of the laity. This will happen if there is not only 'a theology *of* the laity', to quote the title of Kraemer's book, but 'a theology *for* the laity' and 'a theology *by* the laity' as well.

A theology *of* the laity, he warns, involves more than thinking about who the laity are and what their calling is inside and outside the church. Such a topic could simply be appended to the themes of a systematic theology. Instead, the main subjects of such a theology — the doctrine of God, creation, man, salvation, church, sacraments, mission and eschatology — should be re-examined for the implications they have for a theology of the laity. This is what John Macquarrie had begun to do examining the relationship of the people with God, Christ and the Spirit as well as their character, environment and destiny.[7]

Out of this should come a theology *for* the laity. At this

J. Macquarrie, passim. See also N. Pittinger, *The Ministry of All Christians: A Theology of Lay Ministry*, Morehouse-Barlow, 1983.

Compare the approaches of E. Furley, 'Interpreting Situations' and O.S. Browning, 'Practical Theology & Religious Education', Formation and Reglection: The Promise of Practical Theology, *L.S. Mudge & J.N. Poling (eds), Fortress, 1987, pp.11-14, 88-92.*

point Mouw moves quite beyond anything in Macquarrie's work. The agenda for such a theology would not be the clerically-dominated concerns of traditional theological discussion, but the needs, dilemmas and problems of lay people themselves. The goal should be equipping the laity to fulfil their reponsibilities and potential in the world. With the help of a range of biblical metaphors that describe various aspects of the life of the people of God, Mouw underlines the importance of every type of group and organisation and every sphere of human life coming under practical theological scrutiny. But this will only take place if lay people overcome their antipathy to theology — much of it well justified — and engage in a more relevant form of it themselves. For it is only lay people who can help define the main issues that must be addressed and identify the key factors that must be taken into account.

So a theology must be developed *by* the laity as well. If they can develop a new model for their work and the skills to go with it, theologians can also contribute to this. The chief method by which Christians can gain clarity about their responsibilities is through 'discernment'. This enables us to identify the underlying motivations, dispositions and forces at work in society as well as their personal, social and cultural consequences. But discernment, insists Mouw, is essentially a communal act: intuitions, data, hypotheses and proposals that come to lay people from their experience of the world should be shared with the wider Christian community and weighed by it. Since God's presence in the world is a complex and hidden affair, however, insights that come out of this process must be regarded as tentative.

If discernment is the means by which lay people come to understand their responsibility in the world, concern for those most disadvantaged by society should be the main focus of lay attention. The warrant for this concern is the special place the Bible accords to the 'poor'. Mouw has not only the economically poor in mind, but those who are discriminated against legally and politically. People that are significantly disadvantaged today are women and non-whites, though many others are oppressed in some way. Such people may be affluent, privileged and powerful, but still suffer oppression at other levels. Even if our main concern should be for those who are most disadvantaged, we cannot remain unconcerned about the plight of the more 'well-off' members of society.

In his concluding chapter Mouw discusses ways in which people can be best equipped for ministry in the world. It is difficult, he says, to fulfil our role in the world and most people do not feel adequate to do it. There are no simple solutions and our effectiveness depends as much on personal renewal and growth as upon learning how to think and act rightly. Existing programmes of lay education — adult Sunday School classes, senior fellowships, occupationally-based Bible studies, Christian service organisations and social action groups — go only part of the way here. These are meagre in comparison with the resources available for the training of clergy. Lay education programmes are often poorly staffed and planned. Educational goals are often subordinate to other purposes. The issues they discuss only rarely touch upon the role of lay people in the world. Only if they are reconstituted could such structures equip lay people more effectively.

During the last fifteen years a number of organisations have emerged which embody the concerns expressed in Mouw's book. These organisations go beyond those that arose after the Second World War. Indeed, some of them go beyond Mouw's own recommendations. The centres described earlier mostly began in Europe, only later surfacing elsewhere. Their newer counterparts exist mostly in North America, but are now also emerging in other countries. Whereas the earlier centres received support from denominational, business and government sources, the newer institutions have had to finance their operations primarily through fees and gifts. For that reason they sometimes have a more precarious existence than their predecessors. Another difference is that the newer institutions cater almost exclusively for Christians. These dissimilarities partly reflect the non-Established Church environment of most of the new enterprises, as well as their substantial lay origins.

It is encouraging to see that for the most part it was lay people who established these new institutions. In one case this owed much to the Brethren connections of those involved. In another it was due to the Christian counter-culture environment in which the founders largely worked. Elsewhere lay people coming out of a Reformed tradition, with its emphasis on Christ's rule over the whole of life, took the initiative. Unlike the evangelical academies and their later counterparts, these new centres also offer more substantial study programmes. These programmes take different forms in different institutions. Many require a graduate degree as an entrance requirement and either have, or are seeking, academic accreditation. However, others cater for a broader audience and do not offer diplomas or degrees.

In the last six months of 1983 and first six months of 1984 I had the opportunity to visit a number of these institutions. This was not just a tourist exercise. I had learned from experience that the only way to really discern what was taking place was to spend an extended period of time in a place, taking part as fully as possible in its life and hearing the views of those at the grassroots as much as those at the top. I would like to give a brief profile of each institution, beginning with one with which I spent the least time.

The London Institute of Contemporary Christianity is only six or seven years old. It is located in the heart of the city, only a block from the large retail stores on Oxford Road. There a disused chapel has been turned into a teaching space, study and library area and offices. The Institute runs three residential programmes a year, each two months long. No degree is required for admission and no recognised qualification is awarded for work done. The Institute also runs evening courses for people who work in the city and intensive summer-schools for people all over England. There are occasional extension programmes in county capitals. What struck me about the London Institute was its unusual blend of the traditional and experimental. This was symbolised, I felt, by the building in which it meets. While many of the courses break out of the usual pattern, others do not and teaching methods tend to be rather conventional. Worship is integrated with study, though study does not arise very often out of concrete concerns. Yet the Institute has a very cosmopolitan group of students. Most come from the Two-thirds World and this gives all that takes place a cultural diversity and richness less evident elsewhere.

In Vancouver, Canada, Regent College occupies a number of large buildings on the edge of the University of British Columbia. The college began in the late sixties and offers programmes ranging from a one year diploma to a four year Master's degree. With minor exceptions, all but the first programme involve full-time study. The college also runs a summer school programme open to anyone who is interested and has a number of extension courses. Begun as a deliberate attempt to take theology to the people, in terms of numbers Regent College has exceeded all expectations. It is now the largest theological institution anywhere in Canada. It has, in fact, increasingly developed into a kind of lay seminary. Its curriculum, teaching methods and forms of assessment are mostly a modified version of that found in any theological college. What it does at this level it does very well indeed and many students have paid it glowing tributes. It continues to attract a very international clientele. But I wished there had been a more sustained attempt to rethink theological education for the whole people of God in terms of their everyday responsibilities and needs. It is indicative, perhaps, that the majority of the degree students seem to be looking for some type of full-time, church-related work.

I have been fortunate enough to have two separate semester-length stays at New College, Berkeley. This has been in existence for about ten years and rents accommodation from a theological college close to the Berkeley campus of the University of California. At the college, students can undertake a one year part-time diploma course or full-time Master's course in Christian studies, though the latter can also be completed part-time over a longer period. There is also a more intensive two year Master's programme and there are certificate programmes in both campus and cross-cultural ministry.

Any of the courses can be taken by people not pursuing a degree. To make courses more accessible, much of the teaching is conducted in the evenings, on weekends or through intensive summer and winter courses. There are also extension programmes for those living further afield. By far the majority of students at New College are part-time and expect to remain in a secular occupation. Here I experienced a far more communal atmosphere, observed a greater attempt to develop a new type of curriculum more directly related to the average Christian, and found a more concerted effort to help people integrate their growing theological understanding with the particular jobs, interests and commitments they have.

How do these centres differ from more traditional theological institutions? Biblical studies courses are less technical. Historical studies give more attention to the effects of secularisation on modern society and focus more on social, cultural and multicultural concerns. Theological studies focus more on apologetics and on the doctrines of creation and the kingdom of God. More innovation is evident in, and more time is given to, Christian Ethics. There are units on the formation of values, business and professional morality, the ethics of sex and family life, the problems of urban living, and contemporary economic and political issues. A greater range of interdisciplinary programmes opens up a Christian perspective on such matters as world views, academic disciplines, art and society, and the role of the media and science and technology.

In the practical theology area, more room is given to such

concerns as vocation, lay evangelism and spirituality, public discipleship, congregational leadership and the role of women. Most of these institutions also organise weekend conferences on a variety of issues such as unemployment, power and powerlessness in the city, the Christian in the marketplace, faith and art, journal-keeping and life-planning, as well as specialist conferences for a broad range of occupational groups.

Of course, there are many other institutions committed to bringing theology into closer contact with the world of the average Christian. Some, like the Westwood Foundation in Los Angeles or the Discipleship Training Centre in Singapore, are more traditional in their interests or more focussed on training for full-time Christian work. An organisation that seeks to relate theology to life in a more informal and more ideological fashion is the L'Abri Fellowship, which now has centres in England, Holland and Italy as well as in Switzerland. At a post-graduate level an ambitious programme is offered by the Institute of Advanced Studies in Toronto, Canada, where faith is applied to contemporary world views, academic disciplines and socio-political movements.

There are also some denominationally-based Christian education organisations, such as the Albany Institute in Washington and the Elm Centre in Australia, which are geared more to preparing people to take a larger role in congregational life. In a theological college context, there is also the Center for the Ministry of the Laity in Newtown, Massachusetts, and the values programme of the San Francisco Theological Seminary. Residential centres, such as the Lygonier Fellowship in Pennsylvania, the Mackenzie Study Centre in Oregon and the C.S. Lewis Institute in Washington, also intermittently draw people together to reflect on a variety of concerns.

A pioneering approach

According to Richard Mouw, we are still in the second stage of the development of a lay theology. The third stage, he says, will involve the detailed discussion of specific problems. But there is more to the third stage than he suggests and moving into it will involve more novel approaches and institutions than have yet appeared. Still, attention is now beginning to be paid to specific aspects of work or non-work life.

For example, books are starting to deal with such issues as professional ethics, living standards, the use of time and leisure. But there are many areas of daily life that have not yet even surfaced. We are also only beginning to see approaches to theological education which bring this to bear more closely on the everyday concerns of people.

In order to see what the future may hold in this area, we must look away from Europe and North America to the Two-thirds World. If it was in Europe that the first stage of a theology of the people came to the surface, and in North America that new developments in popular theological education first appeared, it is in the Two-thirds World that the move into a third stage is most advanced.

In recent years, theologians and educationalists in the West have turned their attention to this part of the world for two main reasons. Liberation Theology challenged them to redefine the content and method of what they were doing and Theological Education by Extension suggested a new model of training for ministry. Both these movements have opened up the possibility of a more effective translation of Christian convictions into everyday life situations.

Liberation Theology insists that the first step towards real understanding is to look closely at the situation in which we are placed. This situation has to be analysed and all the factors that bear on it must be identified. So the concrete situation, not the biblical text, is the starting point for discerning what God wants of us in that situation. The Bible itself, they would claim, is a record of real people in real situations: it was as they actually confronted these and sought to understand them that God declared his purposes.

The trouble with most theology in the West was its failure

to begin with concrete problems. This was why it was so rarely able to provide any concrete solutions. The widely talked about 'irrelevance' of theology largely stems from this failure. Much of the writing that issued from Liberation Theology, at least in the initial stages, focussed on the general economic, social and political situation in Latin America and tended to be very academic in character. While it challenged the way in which theology was done in the West, it still reflected much of the Western style of communication. The people for whom it was written were mostly an educated elite. The setting in which much of it was done was primarily tertiary institutions. In other words such thinking was often more a theology of the people, rather than by and for the people.

One of the best known of the Liberation theologians, both inside and outside Latin America, is Jean Luis Segundo. I picked up his book, *The Liberation of Theology*, just a few months after I had made the decision to leave the academic world, yet before I had completed my time in it.[8] In a different setting to the Latin American one, I was also feeling my way towards a new model for doing theology. Segundo's book, which I read during a period when considerable pressure was coming my way to stay in the academic world, fell into my hands at the right time.

This is not to say that I always found myself in agreement with it. The illustrations of concrete situations contained in the book seemed too general, the reliance on Marxist analysis too heavy and the style in which it was written too cerebral. But its criticism of the way in which theology has become so professionalised in the West, so confined to a select, well-educated audience and so vested with ecclesiastical interests, was penetrating. Contrast this, says Segundo, with the unprofessional, non-formal and prophetic character of theology among Jesus and the early Christians. What we require is 'the return of theology from the rarefied atmos-

---

8.   J.L. Segundo, *The Liberation of Theology*, Orbis, 1976

phere of academia to the world of common sense'. This 'common sense' has little to do with the prepackaged 'common sense' that is handed out to us through the mass media or in the commonplaces of the consumer society. Segundo lists four marks of such a 'common-sense' theology:
(a) We must move away from an abstract or academic theology to one which grows out of a commitment to change people and improve the world.
(b) We must analyse how society works if we are to take the word of God and convert it from a vague outline to a clearly defined message.
(c) We must avoid stating purely timeless, universal truths and address God's word to specific problems and situations.
(d) We must not bend the word of God to our own ends if we are to say something that is really creative and liberating.[9]

What this means in practice for the people of God is spelled out in Segundo's manual, *A Theology for Artisans of a New Humanity*.[10] In this he covers a number of the main themes of traditional theology, but in a way that is relevant to the situation of people in the Two-thirds World. There are discussions of the church as community, the human condition, ideas of God, the meaning of the sacraments and the notion of guilt. His work takes account of the major intellectual currents of the day and also the social and political situation in Latin America. Although Segundo does not examine the most common, day-to-day activities and concerns of such people, he does relate theology to the pressing social and political problems that they have.

The way in which the material in these volumes has been put together and used is interesting. There are a number of initial reflections interleaved with sections which develop and apply the central ideas more concretely and suggest topics for study. This material can be used in a number of ways, such as full-length courses, study weeks and intensive

---

9. op.cit., p.39
10. J.L. Segundo, *A Theology for Artisans of a New Humanity*, Orbis, 1974.

seminars. It is the last of these formats which he and his colleagues have found most helpful for 'busy lay people'. The latter are encouraged to take part in one seminar a year. This runs over three or four days and is broken up into four-hourly sessions. Those attending are expected to participate fully in the brief periods set aside for general questions, personal meditation, study groups and group reports. The outcome should be a conversation and debate about what people have heard and about their real-life experiences. There is also time at each session for recollection and prayer.

I have discussed Segundo's approach in some detail for it is a vital part of his understanding of theology as a whole. One of the marks of the new stage in a theology of the people is its concern to find alternative ways of developing and disseminating it. However, Segundo's content and practice is mainly relevant to an educated elite. He also tends to begin from his understanding of the situation in which people find themselves rather than from their perception of it. In a more recent paper he admits this and talks about a shift in the work of some Liberation theologians which begins with the people and invites them to become more a part of the theologising process.[11]

Part of the reason for this is that some theologians in Latin America have sought to identify much more with the beliefs as well as aspirations of the people rather than tending to criticise many of these for their superficiality or even superstitious character. More significantly, a number of theologians began to move out of their seminaries for part of the time each year and work among the poorer classes. Here and there some of these thinkers have left the academic world behind altogether and placed themselves at the disposal of the poor and oppressed on the fringes of some of the great cities. This has led to a more people-orientated and people-involved approach to theology, perhaps even one that is too

---

11. J.L. Segundo, 'The Shift Within Latin American Theology', Lecture given at Regent College, Toronto, March 22, 1983

uncritical of certain aspects of the people's values and capacities.

Alongside these theological approaches, and in part overlapping them, there are two models of theological education coming out of the Two-thirds World which have a more grassroots flavour.

First, there is Theological Education by Extension or TEE. This does not draw people out of their local situation to train them for future service but trains them for present service in their actual situation. By this means a greater number of people are able to be involved. With the help of specially prepared materials, these work alone or in groups, with regular visits by teachers.[12] But TEE is primarily geared to people who wish to exercise some ministry in the church. Also, both in content and method, much of it is merely a modified version of the residential theological college curriculum.

There are exceptions to this, such as some of the courses developed in Bangalore, India. Here, even in a course on Christology, students begin by studying the economic, social and political setting in the first century and Jesus' response to it. Then they reflect on their own context and look for common elements between the two. As they let these two horizons interact, they open up a deeper understanding of both. Throughout the course, students work up a case study, evaluate some Christian activity, write their own parables and carry out a practical project.[13]

Second, there is also the more informal learning that takes place in the so-called basic communities in the Two-thirds World.[14] This grassroots church movement among the poor,

---

12. Further to TEE in Latin America see K.B.Mulholland, *Adventures in Training in the Ministry*, Presbyterian and Reformed, 1976
13. Details of this are available from C.Sugden, Oxford Centre for Mission Studies, PO Box 70, Oxford, UK.
14. See now the exhaustive and perceptive analysis by G.Cook, *The Expectation of the Poor: a Protestant Perspective on Base Ecclesial Communities*, Orbis, 1986.

particularly in Catholic areas, has created small, lay-led communities which worship together and engage in social action. This provides a communal and practical setting in which ordinary people can learn to bring faith and life into real contact.

There are an estimated 150,000 of these in Central and Latin America. In the spirit of the Brazilian educationalist Paolo Freire, this involves identifying the actual situation in which disadvantaged members of society find themselves and then reflecting biblically on that situation. Out of this setting, with the help of itinerant 'pastoral agents' who facilitate this process, have come materials that are more geared to the average person than those devised by Segundo. An interesting example of this from Peru has now been published in English.[15]

In these various ways — Segundo's seminars, TEE programmes and grassroots church meetings — we begin to move beyond the second stage of a theology of the people. Each of these enters more fully and more effectively into the area that I have described as 'the theology of everyday life'. In these different settings, there is a real attempt to help people understand why that world is structured the way it is, how it affects their daily lives and what, Christianly speaking, they can do about it. The people themselves are involved in the process of discovering these things and deciding how to respond to them.

In many respects our situation in the West is dissimilar. Everyday life has a different character here and there is a higher level of education. It is important to recognise these differences. Otherwise a naive transfer of Two-thirds World models to Western conditions might be attempted. In any case the whole spirit of the Two-Thirds World approach is against this. Its message is: begin with your own situation and allow the word of God to come into contact with it. Since

---

15. For an example of this educational process at work among poorer groups see V. Caminando, *A Peruvian Catechism* , SCM, 1985

everyday reality for most people in the West is different to that in the Two-thirds World, the theology appropriate to our situation will in some respects be different as well.

In several Western societies, counterparts of the three Latin American approaches I have mentioned do exist. For example, the Urban Theology Unit in Sheffield, England, has developed a methodology and program that borrows heavily from the Liberation Theology model. In doing so it has attracted a great deal of interest, but also provoked a significant degree of opposition. But while it has challenged people's understanding of the concerns and methods of theology, it has carried over too much of the ideological superstructure and definition of the poor from the Two-thirds World. As a result, the Unit's work does not have as everyday a feel about it as it might.

TEE has now spread to many Western countries. In Australia, it has been taken up mainly by the Anglican General Board of Religious Education and the Diocese of Armidale, the Christian and Missionary Alliance churches and, most interestingly, at Nungalinya College, Darwin. The latter is a training institution for Aborigines sponsored by two leading denominations. Though it has a campus to which students come for part of their theological education — to help overcome the fragmentation of Aboriginal society by breaking down tribal barriers — most of the students' time is spent in their original tribal or urban settings. Through regular visits by college staff, help from local part-time tutors, the use of cassettes and highly innovative written materials, a real attempt is being made to relate theology to the actual situations, everyday problems and indigenous aspirations of the Aboriginal people. The extensive use of 'story' as a way of introducing students to the Bible, the incorporation of Aboriginal methods of learning and the emphasis upon work alongside study in the local situation, result in a pioneering approach to theological education.

Over the last twenty years, in the United States, Australia and Great Britain, grassroots church communities have also come into being. There are modified versions of basic communities, mainly located in disadvantaged inner-city areas and often with a middle-class core. While most of these arise within a particular denominational framework, links are often stronger with similar groups in the same area. Intentional communities which both church and work together also exist in many places: some of these are attached to a local church, others operate autonomously. Alternative churches — smaller, more informal, socially aware congregations meeting in basements or rented rooms — are also now a fact of life. Home churches — whether independent, interdenominational or based in a congregation — are also growing.

In all four types of grassroots communities, learning generally centres on the needs and desires of those involved or those whom they are seeking to reach. Concrete situations are frequently the starting point for biblical reflection, prayer and discussion. Everyone participates in this process and learning is a holistic rather than head-orientated affair.

Conclusion
According to Ian Fraser, who has travelled widely and reported on recent trends at the grassroots Christian level:

In much of the world church, the membership is no longer leaving theology to "theologians" but hammering it out at white heat in the fire of experience, tempering it as weaponry for the fights of life.

No longer is a prescribed, largely academic education looked to to fit people for the task. The deficiencies of such an education are now being more and more recognised — the withdrawal from the mainstream of life; the lack of lively contact with the language and daily experience of so many people; the stress on book-knowledge; distance from a variously gifted and involved community in which to test and check insights. The theological training of Jesus, provided in the thick of life, which developed senses alert to the sights, sounds, smells, actions and interactions of life in the streets, in the homes and fields, on the lake; and which depended on wrestling in prayer and with the scriptures to find the mind of the Father, is being appreciated afresh. To training in theological awareness and perceptiveness of this kind, all sorts of people may have access. They are seizing their chance.

No longer is a scholarly caste given the last word in judging what is of worth in the field of theology — how can those sort out wheat from chaff who have never ploughed a field? Scholars can have a part in the whole work. They are no longer allowed to corner the theology market.

Illiterates now make perceptive contribution to the church's theological understanding. Work people on the land and in industry play their part in building up theological resources ... At last theology is being done in community by people with very diverse forms of experience. They provide an essential element which has been missing. Disciplined reflection, which theology requires, must have a richness of doing and perceiving to work on... It takes a community, reflecting deeply on reality as it is experienced, to give theology substance and shape; a community in which every member's contribution is respected and relished as well as critically assessed that it might find its place in a communal perceiving of God and his ways and works.[16]

But there is still a long way to go. What Fraser describes only takes place among a small minority of Christians. In most places it is business as usual. Where it does take place there is often too academic a takeover of theological perspectives and too naive a borrowing from non-Western grassroots models. These models, and the theology that goes with them, are not sufficiently evaluated, corrected and modified in the light of our particular situation and other biblical principles. We need a home-grown approach which has its own distinctive character.*

---

16. I. Fraser, op. cit., pp.4-5

17. For the latest report on emerging forms of theological reflection, primarily in developing countries, see *Theology by the People: Reflections on Doing Theology in Community*, Samuel Amirtham and John S. Pobee (eds), WCC, 1986. The discussion of their implications for theological reflection in developed countries shows how much remains to be done to biblically critique this, to contextualise what is valuable and to translate it into grass roots educational structures. Relevant to this whole question, though not written from a Christian perspective, is the attempt to relate the work of Paolo Freire to ordinary life in I. Shor, *Critical Teaching and Everyday Life*, University of Chicago, 1987.

Appendix B:

Resources and agencies for lay education

IF YOU WISH TO PURSUE any of the steps laid out in the last two chapters of this book, here are some suggestions.

1. If you are in a context which enables you to develop a clearer Christian perspective on everyday life, then your main need is for resources. You might begin by looking at the books in the footnotes to chapter four that are associated with the particular learning context you are in or at those in chapter three that are associated with the particular topic you are interested in. One of these may provide the starting point you require. For each country I have included a few key organisations in different regions, which could help you find out about others.

2. If you are looking for a particular context in which to build up a Christian understanding of everyday life, that is for one of the approaches listed in chapter four, you could contact any one of the following. For each country I have included key organisations in different regions which could make you aware of others closer to your place of residence or particular concern.

Australia:
> Zadok Centre or St Mark's Institute
> Cnr Broughton and Blackall Streets
> Canberra ACT 2600

Elm Centre
PO Box 2148
Parramatta NSW 2151

United Kingdom:
London Institute for Contemporary Christianity
Vere Street
London SW1

Shaftesbury Project
8 Oxford Street
Nottingham NG1 5BH

Canada:
Regent College
2130 Wesbrook Mall
Vancouver BC VT6 1W6

Institute for Christian Studies
229 College Street
Toronto Ontario M5T 1R4

United States:
New College
2600 Dwight Way
Berkeley CA 94704

Center for the Ministry of the Laity
210 Herrick Road
Newtown Center MA 01259

Crossings
c/- 6337 Clayton Road
Saint Louis Miss 63117

Apart from these lay institutes, there are other organisations
which set up occasional short courses or lecture series as part
of a broader programme. These may be attached to colleges,

universities, para-church organisations, grassroots communities or local churches. Throughout North America, Christian liberal arts colleges provide, with varying degrees of specificity, an institutional context for relating faith to everyday life and information about these can be obtained from:

The Christian College Coalition
235 Second Street, NE
WASHINGTON DC 20002

There are also organisations which work among particular occupational groups, seek to deal with some area of life requiring serious attention or undertake research on various contemporary issues.

Details of such organisations in Australia can be found in: Douglas Hynd, *Australian Christianity in Outline: A Statistical Analysis and Directory*, Lancer Press, 1984, pp.103-106, 132-134 and 141-142 especially.

3. If you are seeking materials for a group you wish to commence or in which you are involved, or a resource person to assist you in dealing with a particular topic, apart from the organisations listed above, you could contact the relevant departments of lay and adult education in your own denomination. A list of denominations and other lay agencies around the world committed to the Christian education of ordinary Christians in more substantial ways may be found in any issue of:

Laity Exchange
c/- 311 MacArthur
SAN LEANDRO CA 94577

See, too, the institutions referred to on p.163 of this book.

Information about lay centres in the United Kingdom and Ireland may be obtained from:

Avdenshaw Project
2 Eaton Gate
London SW1

Appendix C:

Discussion Questions

Chapter 1: An intellectual pilgrimage

1. Do you think there can be a theology of sleep? If so, what is yours?

2. How should we divide our responsibilities between work, church and home?

3. What part should sport play in our lives? What is good and bad about sport?

4. If you were in Jan's shoes (pages 16 to 19), what would your vocation be?

5. How can city life serve our life goals better than it does at the moment?

6. What changes do you think there should be in work patterns?

7. What do you find helpful about the author's own pilgrimage referred to on pages 21 to 26?

Chapter 2: The credibility gap

1. How do you apply your belief to your work? What are two specific changes you think you should make?

2. What should our attitude to leisure be? Draw on your own experience and the information on pages 44 to 46.

3. How can we put the Kingdom of God first in our lives when our routine activities place such demands on us?

4. What are examples from your experience of the acquisition impulse, the subtle forms of worldliness and grey rather than black-and-white moral situations? How can they be dealt with?

5. Consider what may hold you back from a full commitment to Christian belief and Christian behaviour. What are some practical steps that can be taken to deal with this?

6. What are some ways we can discuss together everyday matters in church? Are there 'non-religious' activities we can do together?

7. Pages 58 to 60 show that there is often a gap between belief and our way of life. What do you think can be done to integrate the two?

Chapter 3: The texture of daily life

1. What part do busyness, mobility and debt play in your life?

2. 'We need to challenge features of our society which so many people take for granted or regard as inevitable' (page 68). How can conformity, security and regulation be challenged?

3. Make a list of the routine duties you do each day. Are they all necessary? Are there better ways to organise them?

4. Look at the questions on commuting on page 69. If you are a commuter, what changes would you like to make?

5. The author refers to 'the wide-scale idolatry of the car' (page 70). What is the car's proper and improper role in our lives?

6. Take *one* of the five routine aspects of life mentioned on pages 73 to 75 and list four or five questions that you think are important about it from a Christian viewpoint.

7. 'Since work is the main reality for many of us, we test much else that we experience by judgements we form through it' (page 76). Is work your main reality? What affect does it have on the rest of your life?

8. How can our social rituals and activities (pages 84 to 86) be more Christian?

9. How can the home become a substitute religion?

10. 'A doctrine only has power... to the extent to which it creates a style of life' (page 89). Do you agree? What do you find helpful in the statement on page 89 by Jacques Ellul?

Chapter 4: The reality principle

1. Read paragraph 2, page 93 starting 'But we do need . . .'. How should we decide which issues to concentrate on?

2. What advantages does the home church have for developing our theology? Read pages 95 to 97.

3. In what ways is role modelling (pages 97 to 100) valuable?

4. What advantages does a working group (pages 100 to 104) have?

5. What is necessary to make a workshop (pages 104 to 109) work well?

6. Using Wingeier's suggestion of using an experience, not a decision, as a basis for theology (page 110), write down an experience and share and discuss it with your group along the lines suggested on pages 110 to 112.

7. Dilemmas for most Christians from everyday life are often as 'intricate, subtle and perplexing' as the issues that fill traditional theological textbooks. Share some issues that have arisen for you from being a Christian in the world.

Chapter 5: A people's theology

1. If it is true that theologians often 'reside in a kind of ecclesiastical academy' (page 121), how does this affect their knowledge and vision?

2. Take one area of your life — economics, for example — and share with others the theology that lies behind your thoughts and ideas in that area.

3. Give an example of an ethical problem where the lay Christian is more likely to have expertise than the professional theologian.

4. How has your experience of life enabled you to 'know' some theological point in the sense in which the author uses the term 'know' on page 130?

5. 'We are in danger of over-stressing the role of the intellect in our lives' (page 131). What aspects other than the intellect are important? Why are they important?

6. Take one of the doctrines discussed on pages 135 to 139 and show how it relates to your workplace and everyday routine.

7. How can you best equip yourself to be a theologian?